SEARCHING FOR MY MISSING FATHER

AN AMERICAN NOIR

ALLISON DREW

Black Rose Writing | Texas

©2020 by Allison Drew
All rights reserved. No part of this book may be reproduced, stored in a retrieval system or transmitted in any form or by any means without the prior written permission of the publishers, except by a reviewer who may quote brief passages in a review to be printed in a newspaper, magazine or journal.

The author grants the final approval for this literary material.

First printing

This is a work of non-fiction. Some names have been changed.

ISBN: 978-1-68433-537-4
PUBLISHED BY BLACK ROSE WRITING
www.blackrosewriting.com

Printed in the United States of America
Suggested Retail Price (SRP) $18.95

Searching for my Missing Father is printed in Sabon

*As a planet-friendly publisher, Black Rose Writing does its best to eliminate unnecessary waste to reduce paper usage and energy costs, while never compromising the reading experience. As a result, the final word count vs. page count may not meet common expectations.

For all missing persons and those who miss them.

ACKNOWLEDGEMENTS

My sincere thanks to those who have read and commented on part or all of this manuscript over the course of its many drafts.

At the outset I benefitted tremendously from an online memoir writing course with Mary-Jane Holmes of Fish Publishing. I am extremely grateful to Connie DiBiasio, Bettina Drew, Karl French, David Howell, James Kilgore, Jack Mapanje, and Claire O'Kell for reading and commenting on portions of the manuscript and, especially, to Linda Greenow, David Johnson, the late Eudora Kombo, Carolyn Levin and Elaine Mokhtefi for reading the entire manuscript. Peter Bricklebank gave much useful advice. Thanks also to Betty, Christine, Jean, Pearl and Serena at Writers Together in York, who listened to readings from early drafts. Donald Connery and Michael Dooling offered very thoughtful comments about my father's vanishing and the state police investigation.

On the history of Connecticut's northwest corner I am very grateful to Katherine Chilcoat, former Town Historian, Salisbury Association, and to Paul Grant-Costa and Tobias Glaza, editors of the Yale Indian Papers Project.

From June 14-16, 2017, I attended the Third International Conference on Missing Children and Adults held at Abertay University in Dundee, Scotland. The conference had a profound impact on me. Until then, virtually the only people I encountered who were genuinely concerned with missing persons were their family members or very close friends. At the conference I met for the first time a range of professionals who were seriously concerned with missing persons and who had reflected deeply about the impact of missing persons on those left behind. It was also the first time, aside from one or two rare individuals, that anyone truly took my experiences and feelings about being connected to a missing person seriously and showed any interest in learning about my experiences. At the plenary session I read a brief selection entitled "Missing!" from my draft memoir. The conference helped me tremendously. I am extremely grateful to all the conference organizers and participants and thank them all very much.

Finally, many thanks to Reagan Rothe and the Black Rose Writing team for their belief in this project.

SEARCHING FOR MY MISSING FATHER

PREFACE

This memoir concerns the vanishing of my father, Thomas Pendleton Drew, my efforts to discover what happened to him and the psychological impact of both on me.

My reconstruction of the events concerning my father's disappearance and the ensuing Connecticut State Police investigation is based overwhelmingly on police and court records and other primary sources in the public domain. Many of these records were obtained under Connecticut's Freedom of Information Act. The court records include the depositions of two of my father's employees and the divorce records of one of his employees. Through my academic work I have developed expertise in the use of documentary evidence and interviews, methods that form the backbone of my memoir.

This is a work of non-fiction. Some names have been changed. Conversations between myself and others have been reproduced based on notes made at the time or on emails. Occasionally, I have recreated conversations based on my recollections of past events. As with any historical work, I have endeavored to be as factually accurate and truthful as possible. The views and opinions expressed here, informed by my research and interpretations of the facts, are my own. My father's disappearance remains unresolved.

Perhaps unsurprisingly, the non-fiction literature on police investigations of missing persons is scanty. Two exceptions are Michael C. Dooling, *Clueless in New England: The unsolved disappearances of Paula Welden, Connie Smith and Katherine Hull*, Carrollton, 2010 and Carole Moore, *The Last Place You'd Look: True stories of missing persons and the people who search for them*, Rowman & Littlefield, 2011. James Joyce's story "The Dead" helped me to reflect on the differences between deceased and missing persons.

Despite its small, seemingly low-crime communities, Connecticut's northwest corner has generated a number of mystery and true crime books. The Belgian author Georges Simenon lived in Lakeville in the early 1950s and wrote two novels set in the area: *La Mort de Belle* [1951], translated as *Belle* in *Tidal Wave*, Doubleday, 1954, pp. 9-132, and *La Main* [1968], translated as *The Man on the Bench in the Barn*, 1969 and *The Hand*, Penguin, 2016. *Belle* and *The Hand* dissect the social mores of a fictional Salisbury, eerily presaging the northwest corner's later real-life crimes.

The following non-fiction books have provided important background on and insights into the varied relationships between the Connecticut State Police and the northwest corner communities. Mildred Savage, *A Great Fall: A murder and its consequences*, Simon and Schuster, 1970, set in Barkhamsted, concerns the 1965 murder of Dorothy Thompsen, the confession of her mentally-ill mother-in-law and the later forced confession of Harry Solberg. The murder investigation is set against the intense factionalism of the state police. The 1973 murder of Barbara Gibbons and the state police rush to judgment of her son Peter Reilly is the subject of two books: Joan Barthel, *A Death in Canaan: A classic case of good and evil in a small New England town*, [1976] Open Road Media, 2016, and Donald S. Connery, *Guilty Until Proven Innocent* [1977] Berkley Mass Market, 2010. Arthur Herzog, *A Murder in Our Town: A true crime story*, iUniverse Star, 2004, concerns the August 1985 burning of the Salisbury Town Hall and the October 1986 murder of witness Earl Morey. Finally, Dooling's *Clueless*, mentioned above, assesses the Connecticut State Police response to Connie Smith's 1952 vanishing from Lakeville.

My memoir follows in their tradition.

PROLOGUE

I once heard an African fable about a turtle who, wandering along a forest path, had the misfortune of encountering a leopard. Knowing it was doomed, the turtle made one final request, which the leopard magnanimously granted. The turtle then began furiously scratching the soil, strewing it all about. Puzzled, the leopard asked the turtle what it was doing.

"After you have killed me," it replied, "I want everyone passing by here to see that I struggled."

I am the turtle.

CHAPTER 1

York, England, July 2007
Sitting at my desk, Margo purring on my lap, I call Daddy in Salisbury, Connecticut.

"Hey Daddy."

"Hello darlin'. How is ... England?"

"England's fine, Daddy. How are you? The place must look lovely."

"It surely does. When're you coming home, darlin'?"

"Daddy, I'll be there in September, for my birthday."

In the silence that follows I sense his disappointment.

What I don't yet know is that this will be our last conversation. Two weeks later, Daddy, ninety-one, frail and short of breath, would vanish into thin air, like a fragile fall leaf buffeted by the wind into nothingness.

• • •

Salisbury, Connecticut
Here, deer grazed tranquilly, darting off when they spied a human; wild turkeys paraded with their young, scurrying away at a human's approach; the occasional bear lumbered through, unconcerned. As always, when I passed through the two white pillars marking Daddy's land and rounded the bend, a warm wave swept through me.

A pale yellow French Colonial style stucco house, ivy creeping up its walls, stood in the middle of an expansive lawn. The house was edged in pachysandra, and manicured hedges bordered the white-graveled driveway near the garage. The lawn was enclosed by walls of green—shimmering woods on the far right, shadowy pines on the far left, and far ahead, the still deeper green Berkshire Mountains. A large locust tree stood in front of the house. The lawn was stylized with a rectangular white gravel path bounded at each corner by fir trees grown far beyond their expected size.

Their first spring here Mommy planted petunias. Some seeds slipped through her fingers onto the graveled path. The petunias multiplied each year, blooming so profusely that the white path would be covered with a carpet of pulsating magenta, as it was now. Those petunias signaled Mommy's spirit, her artless gesture softening the formalism, as did the apple trees dotting the lawn.

Out back three silver elms stood in a row. The back patio steps led to another graveled path with peach and cherry blossom trees on either side. Halfway across the lawn an armillary sundial Mommy found in an antique store stood in the middle of her herb garden. The path continued to Daddy's long overgrown fenced vegetable garden. Behind that, where woods began, was the remnant of a low stone wall buried by time—a few moss-covered stones scattered alongside—now a mound offering no hint of what it had once walled in.

Stepping out of the car, I inhaled the scent of pine. When my parents first arrived, their curmudgeonly neighbor Otto, jealously protecting his privacy, planted a row of tiny pines. They became a forty-foot-high grove. To be fair, we appreciated the seclusion and, however cantankerous, Otto helped us during crises, digging Daddy's car out of a snow drift and driving him to the hospital when he had pneumonia.

Then I remembered why I was here.

"*Your father's missing.*"

Daddy's live-in Senior Companion Matt had called me early Sunday morning—middle of the night, his time.

"The police and volunteers have been searching and expect to find him soon."

"What?" I sat up in bed, jostling Margo, who meowed her irritation before falling back asleep. "I don't understand."

I heard Matt inhale.

"Pamela ... Pamela was filling in for me yesterday. She said Tom went outside after dinner. She said around 7:20, while she was watching TV. She said she checked five minutes later and couldn't find him. Anna and I got back at 7:30. We searched but couldn't find him. So we ... I called the police."

Saturday evening, July 21, I reflected mutely.

A creature of habit, Daddy never went out after dinner, and he couldn't have gone far in five minutes.

Over the past year Daddy had become slower and frailer, which was why in the autumn Matt had hired three part-time women to fill in for him. One of them, Pamela, forty-something—Matt had told me over the phone—had gone to Vassar.

"She raised four children and cared for her mother, who had dementia," he said. "And she's just finished a six-week health aide course at Fairview Commons Nursing and Rehabilitation Center, with a 96 GPA."

"Well, her background seems fine. Did you check their references, Matt?"

"Yes, and I know one of them. Karen Kisslinger ... she recommended Pamela. Karen and I go to the same music group. She's a community activist."

Reassured by this, and knowing what a great job he had been doing with Daddy, I didn't ask Matt to send me the list of referees. No point ruffling his feathers.

My first fateful error.

"Have you checked the vegetable garden behind the house? He might have fallen there."

"Yes, they've checked there. I didn't call before because I didn't want to wake you." Why did I accept that, I wonder now? I sat in bed, baffled, trying to grasp the situation.

"I'll talk to you later Matt," I said, feeling numb, disoriented.

Swayed by Matt, watching Margo's chest rise and fall as she slept beside me, I got up and made coffee, waiting almost an hour to call my younger sister Bettina in Missouri.

She had just spoken to Daddy that Friday. He seemed fine, she said.

That afternoon, when I called Matt to see if they'd found Daddy, a woman answered the phone.

"Who's this?" I demanded.

"Pamela."

Pamela?

"You shouldn't be in our home! Please put Matt on the phone. *Now.*"

"Hello Allison."

"Why is Pamela in the house? Why is she answering our phone?"

"She ... I came downstairs and found her in the house. She hadn't rung the bell. I asked her what she was doing here. But the police arrived and started asking her questions, so she stayed. She went upstairs to send a fax."

"She has no right entering our home without permission. She has no business being in our home and sending faxes. She must leave. You must make sure she leaves. She lost our father."

My heart was pounding.

An hour later, I called back.

"The detective wants to talk to you and Bettina," Matt said, sounding irritated.

"Do you have his number?"

"No."

I knew then that I had to fly over. I packed my computer and dragged my suitcase from the closet but couldn't figure out what to put in it ... my mind was whirring non-stop.

Jack, my best friend, my former partner, came to help and to collect Margo. Tall, fair, silvery hair and blue button eyes like those of a teddy bear, Jack knew Daddy well: we had gone to Salisbury together and later, when Daddy visited us, Jack had taken him to Castle Howard—the highlight of his trip.

"Be brave. He'll turn up." He hugged me.

Sunday night, no sleep, I missed the Monday flight. Another sleepless night, stunned by the searchers' inability to find Daddy—some of them worked without sleep those first few nights. Caught the Tuesday morning flight.

Tuesday evening. I turned to the house.

My parents, both artists, designed it. Mommy, a painter and interior decorator, drew up the blueprint. I recall Mommy and Daddy sitting heads together over the blueprint, engrossed in their own creative world. When the house was built, Mommy painted flowers and marbleized designs on the floors, and Daddy, a former fashion designer, wallpapered, sewed the drapes, designed the formal garden and built the slate patios. It was a house of creativity, my parents with their paint brushes and needles, and Bettina and I, when we visited, with our pens and laptops.

But Mommy passed away two years after the house was finished. Shortly after moving to Connecticut, she was diagnosed with cancer. Her New York surgeon didn't provide follow-up care. Later, her Salisbury GP dismissed her claims of feeling unwell and wrote to the other local GPs, describing Mommy as a bored housewife bent on complaining and urging them not to see her. When she was eventually examined, the x-ray showed that the cancer had returned and spread to both lungs. Soon it invaded her brain. When Daddy called the ambulance to take Mommy to the hospital, one of the men, standing near her, called out loudly to his colleague that the doctor had said not to resuscitate her if she died in the ambulance—Mommy heard.

Looking back, I wonder if that cruelty was a harbinger of things to come. But Daddy was determined to put those appalling acts behind him. Before Mommy died he acquired a pointy-faced seal point Siamese cat named Bootsie, and when Bootsie grew old, he adopted a round-faced seal point named Dandy. For more than twenty years, companioned by his cats, Daddy lovingly, single-handedly groomed those grounds.

• • •

I entered through the garage, stepping into the library with its forest green walls and built-in white bookcases. A well-to-do home full of objects carefully collected and placed to express visual beauty. The dark green leather couch and marble coffee table were offset by a white marble fireplace. The French window looked out to the front. Small and cozy, especially in the winter when we lit a fire, it was the most lived-in room. Out of habit I went straight to the caller ID attached to the phone, which listed all incoming calls, answered and missed. To my surprise, no calls were listed for the Saturday or Sunday, although calls for the preceding and following days were listed—how odd.

"Hi Allison. You made it."

Bettina looked tired and disheveled. We were recognizably sisters, although she was slightly bigger, with Daddy's nose, straight light brown hair and light blue eyes, while I had Mommy's nose, wavy hair and smaller dark blue eyes. But our voices were uncannily similar.

We pecked.

"Did you delete the caller ID, Bettina?"

Before she could answer, Matt appeared. A tall, curly-haired kind-faced man in his late fifties, Matt had been working as my father's carer for a year and a half. When he arrived for the job interview in a jacket and tie, he and Daddy had an instant rapport. As Matt was leaving, Daddy impulsively grabbed his hand and kissed it. Matt's face softened.

When Matt drove off, I turned to Daddy.

"Now, do you remember his name?" He stared at me for several seconds.

"Mr Friend."

And that's what he became.

Matt moved in gradually over the coming months. His girlfriend Anna, sixty, worked at the Mary Manning Walsh Nursing Home in Manhattan. She came up every other weekend, and Matt spent alternate Saturday nights with her in Manhattan.

Whenever I called Daddy, he was content, enjoying Matt's company. They shopped and ran errands together: Matt tried to ensure that they drove to town every day.

I had come to see Matt as a friend and expected to stay in touch with him when Daddy passed away.

But now here he was, unable to explain why or how Daddy had disappeared.

"Matt, do you know anything about the caller ID?"

He shook his head. Neither of them knew anything about the missing caller ID numbers.

Yet I knew there'd been many calls. Daddy's youngest sister Mildred had called from Rockmart, Georgia around mid-day on Saturday. A loquacious octogenarian and classical music lover, Mildred collected documents about our ancestors and relayed the family news by phone. She generally spoke to Daddy and Matt three or four times a week. Connecticut state troopers, instructed to look out for an elderly man on foot, had been in and out of the house on Saturday evening and Sunday, using the landline because of poor cell phone reception. Bettina and I had each called several times on Sunday.

Pondering the deleted caller ID numbers, I meandered out of the library through the marble-floored entrance hall and into the pale yellow living room. Light flowed in through six French windows and a row of sliding glass doors, which opened onto the back patio. A large white marble coffee table stood on one of Daddy's needlepoint rugs in front of a black marble fireplace. I stared at his prized painting—the white-domed *Sacré-Coeur Basilica* in Montmartre, Paris by French Impressionist Maxime Maufra, a small brass plaque with the artist's name marking its importance.

Where are you, Daddy?

Through a window, I saw the side patio with its grape arbor. The lawn sloped gently down to a wooded copse leading to the stream where Bettina and I skinny-dipped. I passed through the dining room with its antique table and into the spic and span white kitchen. These rooms also had sliding glass doors overlooking the back.

Two small plastic containers with Daddy's morning and evening pills sat on the lime-green kitchen table. Each container had seven tabs labelled for the days of the week. To avoid confusion, once Daddy took his pills, the tab for that particular day would be left open. The tab for Saturday dinner was closed, but when I checked, the pills were missing.

My gaze moved towards the trash can. Instinct told me to dump the trash on the kitchen floor and check to see if Daddy's pills were in there.

Don't be so paranoid, a little voice chided; I ignored my instinct.

Exhausted by the flight, I trudged upstairs. The bedrooms had smaller windows and walls that sloped in like a cottage. Bettina had taken over Daddy's bedroom. Matt insisted on changing the bedsheets in the guest room where Pamela had slept.

Dazed, I didn't care about sheets. But two months later, when I was leaving to return to England, I would find a used condom at the bottom of the bathroom trash bin. Had Daddy discovered Pamela having sex with someone? Did they argue?

• • •

Wednesday morning I woke early and plodded downstairs to find Matt standing at the kitchen sink.

I looked up at him.

"Matt, please tell me again what happened."

"Pamela said he left around 7:20."

"How do we know she's telling the truth?" I searched his face for an answer. "How could this woman have lost him?"

"I'd been planning to replace her." He flung up his hands. "I gave her a warning last week. I told her she wasn't paying enough attention to Tom. She had *personal* problems. Problems with her husband. I think he called the police on her."

"Matt." I spoke slowly, deliberately. "No one with such personal problems should be looking after a vulnerable person."

"Well, from what I understand," he offered his opinion, "her husband was no angel. She often tried to stay over just to avoid him. In fact, sometimes I found it hard to get rid of her."

My heart sank.

Whoever this woman Pamela was, she had somehow sucked Matt into her personal dramas—at Daddy's expense.

"I would have come back sooner if I'd known things were out of control."

Matt shut his eyes, shaking his head back and forth. "I thought everything *was* under control."

He added that he and the first trooper to arrive on Saturday evening had crossed Daddy's back lawn and walked part-way up the Massachusetts conservation road—a dirt road that bordered Daddy's property and formed the state boundary. They could still see, but the light was dimming, and the trooper swung his flashlight back and forth, noting no signs of a recent passage—no footprints, no trampled earth, no broken twigs or branches.

Daddy, Mommy, Bettina and I had stumbled across the conservation road by chance our first winter at the house, our boots crunching through the thin crust of snow. The road was blocked off with chains at both ends, strewn with fallen trees, accessible only to hikers, horseback riders and occasional cross-country skiers. And joggers—I would later jog along it, past woods with velvety moss terrain and, nearing water, tall rustling reeds topped with feathery plumes. It led to a small cement bridge inscribed "Ravinehurst 1928," and we paused there, speculating at this small monument of history, awed by the icy landscape surrounding us. Across the bridge the road meandered through a pine forest and ended at a small neglected airstrip.

But when Matt and the trooper walked up the road that Saturday evening, the area near the bridge was so overgrown they'd had to turn back.

Two reporters from the *Register Citizen*, a man and a woman, arrived soon after. Trim twenty-somethings, they looked as if they'd stepped out of an *L. L. Bean* clothing catalog. Bettina was still upstairs, so I asked Matt to join us. We went to the dining room and stood near the table, which I had just set up as our search command post with a copy of Matt's statement to the police. Asked about Daddy's daily activities, Matt mentioned reading aloud to help him with his articulation; their latest book was Marguerite Yourcenar's *Memoirs of Hadrian*. Daddy would read a paragraph slowly, haltingly, and Matt would have him repeat the difficult words.

"Perhaps you could tell us about his last day," the woman prompted.

"It was Matt's day off. My father was being looked after by ..."

I was about to mention Pamela's name when I saw Matt gesturing in a downward dismissive motion, as if shooing away a gnat.

"... a fill-in," Matt finished. Stunned, silenced, I imagined the woman who'd been the *last known* person to see Daddy as Marilyn Monroe: a beautiful curvaceous blonde with devastating allure. Why else would Matt have been sucked into her personal dramas and seek to shield her?

The article that appeared the next day would report that Daddy, "went missing from his home ... after telling his part-time caregiver he was going for a walk." They'd accepted the claim Matt relayed as fact. Later that week Pamela would email Matt and thank him for not revealing her name. This we would only learn the next year, when we deposed her and obtained her emails, including one from Matt:

"Stay clear of the house unless you want a confrontation with Allison. Everyone is having a hard time figuring out how Tom got so far away within the 10-15 minute time frame. The conclusion is that you are not being accurate."

The reporters left. The phone rang. More reporters, most arranging times to visit. The *Lakeville Journal* reporter handling the newsbeat from nearby Falls Village where Pamela grew up phoned and asked a few questions but never bothered to visit. Troopers were going in and out of the house. I left messages for the detectives.

I went upstairs to see Bettina, lying listlessly in bed.

"How're you doing?" I perched beside her. Only years later, when I read about the impact of having a missing relative, would I realize that my endlessly whirring thoughts and her lethargy were signs of the shock of learning that a family member is missing. Anger, anxiety and distress, guilt and confusion, stress and sleeplessness are other symptoms. Many people experience depression, post-traumatic stress disorder and prolonged grief disorder, which differs from the grief of bereavement in its higher intensity and longer duration. Psychologist Pauline Boss coined the term *ambiguous loss* to describe the experience. Scanty information and continuing uncertainty about the missing person makes it "the most distressful of all losses," Boss explains, precisely because there is no certitude, no closure.

"Did I tell you I found Dandy cowering in the closet when I arrived," Bettina asked. After Bootsie died, Dandy was Daddy's only cat.

"She's a witness," I replied. "If only she could speak."

Bettina had watched while the Connecticut Canine Search and Rescue team examined the house. This non-profit organization responds to emergency service appeals for lost, missing or drowned persons. The canine handlers were justifiably proud of their animals. Each dog undergoes a two-year training program for each skill—whether finding living humans, cadavers, bodies in water or wild animals—and cross-trained dogs take multiple two-year courses. They can even detect human remains buried a hundred years earlier.

"The dogs behaved oddly when they entered Daddy's bedroom. They kept barking at the windows overlooking the woods," Bettina said slowly. We weren't sure what to make of that. The dogs' behavior and the condom I would find were the only bits of evidence that first summer that something might have happened inside the house.

Did Daddy and Pamela argue near that window? I can hear him now: *This is my home. I want you to leave.*

Maybe they fought. Maybe someone shoved him. Maybe he fell.

Maybe that's what happened.

CHAPTER 2

Two detectives arrived later Wednesday morning. Their crisp, award-winning uniforms signaled professionalism; their badges, authority; their guns, power. Detective Ned Warren, late twenties, fair-skinned, dark-haired, dashingly handsome and smiling, had an earnest and sincere air that made me want to trust him. He said he had been assigned to the case the day after Daddy was reported missing and that his colleague Detective Alex Sorrento—older, taller and unsmiling—would be assisting.

Bettina came downstairs, and the four of us sat around the dining room table. Like many of Connecticut's small rural towns, Salisbury does not have its own police force so relies on the Connecticut State Police, established in 1903 with five troopers. The early troopers spent most of their time travelling across the state to wipe out moonshine, although local lore has it that during Prohibition you could always get a drink in rural Litchfield County. Currently, with twelve barracks, the state police is the main law enforcement agency for half the state's municipalities. Troop B is responsible for northwest Connecticut. Salisbury has one resident trooper, paid partly by the state police and partly by the town.

Detective Warren began describing their search activities, his colleague sitting silently. The first night a police bloodhound had picked up Daddy's scent from his back patio, across the back lawn, through a very short wooded trail, then turning right and heading up the conservation road—exactly where Matt and the trooper had walked a few hours earlier.

Later, I would call the bloodhound handler, who told me he had arrived with the bloodhound at 11:37 pm. The bloodhound crossed the Ravinehurst bridge, his handler recounted, veered off the main path, climbed a twisty trail to a house on Taconic Road, and then lost the scent. The hound followed this route twice. The handler hadn't filed a report because the dog hadn't found anything tangible.

But could Daddy have accomplished such a strenuous hike?

"You needed a machete to get through there. It was virtually impassable, especially around the bridge. There's no way a 91-year-old could have got through," one searcher averred.

That first night another trooper, accompanied by the resident of the Taconic Road house and her neighbor, hiked down from that house before the bloodhound arrived. They, too, found the conservation road virtually impassable. I could only surmise that the bloodhound picked up *their* scent at the bridge and followed it back to that house.

Indeed, the Monday after the disappearance a Connecticut Canine Search and Rescue dog also picked up Daddy's scent on the conservation road, but only as far as the bridge. I was told the scent would have lasted five days. So perhaps Daddy tried going up the conservation road on the Saturday or a few days before, and, exhausted, turned back.

"It's very unusual not to find a missing elderly person when the police arrive so promptly following the report," Detective Warren continued. "We had a case where a husband and wife were in their garden. The wife had dementia. The husband went inside to make lunch, and when he came back with sandwiches a few minutes later, she was gone. He was convinced she couldn't have gone far because she had cardio-pulmonary disease. We found her a few hours later. She'd walked into a shop several miles away." I had heard of this incident.

"That woman was in her 70s, and they found her within a few hours. My father's ninety-one and frail. He has to rest on furniture when he crosses a room."

The detective sat impassively.

"Someone deleted our caller ID for July 21st and 22nd," I added. "Do you know who did this?"

He didn't reply, so I tried again.

"Can you ask Pamela? She entered our home on Sunday. She could have deleted the numbers while Matt was still upstairs."

I spoke again, needing to fill the silence.

"Do you know Pamela?"

Detective Warren nodded.

"She and her husband are from well-known local families. Her sister is a town clerk."

So Pamela was a *local*. She and her siblings—one of them a long-serving town clerk—had grown up in the area, as had her husband. At the time I didn't realize how influential the seemingly modest position of town clerk was: "the hub of government, the direct link between the inhabitants of their community and their government ... the historian of the community," according to the Connecticut Town Clerks Association.

"How can I help?" I asked Detective Warren.

What about distributing flyers, he suggested. We agreed that I would design a flyer and the police would make copies for me.

We were interrupted by the crackle of walkie-talkies. The detectives were called away. We accompanied them outside, and before they left, Detective Warren asked me for a DNA sample. I don't know why they wanted it—they already had items with Daddy's DNA—but dazed by events, I obligingly let him scrape the inside of my cheek with a small stick that he then put inside a tube.

After they left I quickly designed and printed a *Have you seen this man?* flyer with a large photo of Daddy's face. It shows a serious grey-and white-haired old man with a slightly pink complexion, lips pressed together. Wearing a maroon and white cable-knit sweater over a maroon shirt, he gazes directly into the camera with beseeching blue eyes. Bettina couldn't bear to look at those eyes. I dropped it off at Troop B, and a trooper came by later with a box of 500 flyers bearing their logo.

That afternoon I was sitting on the library couch when the phone rang.

"This is Pamela. You owe me $50." My jaw dropped open. *How could she demand money? Why would she?*

"Your sister said she'd send me a check. I'm calling to leave my address so she can send it." Her voice, insistent, whining, unnerved me.

I found my voice.

"You should have gone with him." I accepted the possibility that he left on foot, but I already had doubts. I found her claim that he had vanished within ten minutes and just before Matt returned simply too pat.

"Well, we all know that," she said and hung up.

I remained sitting, stunned at this latest development.

Matt appeared, heading towards the garage.

"That was Pamela," I said. "She claims we owe her money."

Matt stood stiffly, shoulders back, arms at his sides.

"She insisted on being paid before she left."

The check records showed he had paid her for fourteen hours, from 9:30 am when she had allegedly arrived until 11:30 pm, several hours after the police had arrived.

"Why, Matt?" I confronted him. "She *lost* our father. We don't even know how long she was at the house. She might have gone out and left him alone, for all we know."

"I thought I was giving her a *final* check. I wanted her out of the house. She was making a scene. Anna told me to get rid of her. She asked for another $50 and waived some sort of receipt in front of my nose, but I hadn't asked her to buy anything, so I told her to get out."

Generally, Matt did the shopping and prepared dinner. Otherwise, he spent much of his time in his room, which had an air conditioner. Perhaps he was brooding, perhaps he was online, searching for another job.

Thursday morning I found him in the kitchen, gazing across the lawn.

"I keep expecting to see Tom coming across the lawn," he remarked, then turned to me.

"Tom didn't take his Saturday dinner-time pills, Allison." I stared at him.

"How do you know?"

"Because the tab is closed." He checked the pill tray, then realized that although the tab was shut, the pills were gone. I knew that, but why hadn't he mentioned it earlier? Or had it just occurred to him then? Was there anything else he had noticed but not mentioned?

Soon after I set out with the flyers. Returning drained, dehydrated and sweaty late that afternoon, I sat at my desk and called Detective Warren. I still didn't know how Daddy had disappeared. I wanted to pin him down.

"Can you tell me exactly what Pamela said happened Saturday evening?" The detective cleared his throat.

"She said they were watching TV after dinner, a movie called *Too Young to Marry*. She was on the couch, and he was in a chair." I scribbled this down on my notepad. "He got up and said, 'I've got to get going.' He came back a few minutes later wearing a *tan jacket* and sat down. Then he left again. She continued watching TV."

"That's it?"

"Yes."

I ended the call, rushed downstairs and opened the hall closet, pushing the clothes hangers aside one by one. None of Daddy's jackets were missing. I called out to Bettina and Matt.

"Which of Daddy's jackets is missing? What jacket was he wearing that evening, Matt?"

They came to the closet and looked.

"None of them are missing," they both replied.

"Matt, didn't your statement to the police say my father was wearing a tan jacket?"

"The police told me Pamela said he was wearing a tan jacket, so that's what I put."

"Why didn't anyone check the closet?"

"I just assumed if that's what she said, that's what happened."

Daddy loved clothes. A stylish dresser, he took great pleasure in choosing what to wear, whether it was jeans and casual pullover or more formal attire, usually a jacket and tie, when he went to church, to dine out or to volunteer. He dressed more slowly than he had, but he still dressed appropriately. Matt told me that when he left the house on Saturday, Daddy said he wanted to go to church the next day, and Matt reminded him to plan his outfit. If Daddy had chosen to put on a jacket that Saturday evening, there would have been a reason for it—unlikely, given the heat. But, crucially, no jacket was missing.

Now Matt mentioned that Daddy was wearing loose-fitting slip-on shoes.

"He often slipped out of them when he walked, but he liked them and insisted on wearing them."

If Daddy had ambled off and collapsed or gotten lost, surely the police would have found a shoe, at the very least.

It was after 5 pm, so I emailed Detective Warren.

Friday morning Detectives Warren and Sorrento arrived after breakfast. Looking through the hall closet, Detective Warren questioned us in detail about Daddy's jackets. It seemed to me he believed this was an important point that conflicted with Pamela's account. The two detectives then took Matt outside and grilled him for a good twenty minutes.

When they left, Matt came inside shaking his head:

"I'm not going to cover for her, I'm not going to cover for her," he was muttering, before disappearing into his bedroom.

"Matt," I called out, but perhaps he didn't hear me. Cover for what?

Instinctively, I had begun looking for evidence and double-checking claims. Detective Warren had confirmed that the movie Pamela mentioned was showing that Saturday evening. I double-checked. The movie had been shown regularly for a month before the disappearance. She could have watched it anytime—it hardly seemed an alibi for the evening Daddy was reported missing. Yet, according to the police records that I later received, first from Detective Warren and then through the Freedom of Information Act, the police didn't challenge her on this point. Had they done so, there should have been a record in the files that were accessible to me.

Only the next year, when we deposed Pamela, would I finally piece together the events of that evening. When Matt and Anna arrived around 7:30 and found Daddy missing, they both went looking for him. Matt returned thirty minutes later and found Pamela and Anna praying in the library.

"Are you crazy?" he exploded. "You should be searching, not praying!" Anna, an experienced health care professional, should have called the police immediately—after all, Daddy might have fallen and broken a bone. But Pamela demanded attention, so Anna prayed with her.

They agreed they had to call the cops.

"It's going to take them time to get over here. They always have to write everything down," Pamela told the others. "We have got to get right on this." The phrase leapt at me when I read her deposition: get right on what?

They argued about who should phone. Pamela refused.

"I have a very, very conflicted marriage, and we have already had police involved. I just don't want to be the—you know, publicized. My husband will use that against me."

Matt finally phoned at 8:14 pm—twenty-six hours after Bettina's call to Daddy.

The first trooper arrived around 8:30, although his report mistakenly said 8 pm. Matt explained Daddy couldn't walk far due to his breathlessness and slow gait. He had severe cardio-pulmonary disease and used oxygen as needed. He would be out of breath and red in the face by the time he reached the vehicle bridge a few hundred yards from his front door that led to Ravine Ridge Road, a private semi-paved road leading to Route 41. While noting Daddy's "limited mobility ... reducing his movement to a shuffle type gait," the Initial Missing Person report filed on July 23 nonetheless listed "walked off property" as the "cause of absence," never challenging Pamela's claim.

Friday afternoon I sat on the library couch resting, thoughts floating randomly through my mind. The phone rang.

"This is Pamela. I'm calling to remind you about the $50 you owe me and to let you know I'll be out of town this weekend."

CHAPTER 3

In the late 1970s, when my parents were thinking of retiring to the country, they drove through Salisbury. The town claims its name from Salisbury, England; the Scoville Memorial Library—the country's first public library—boasts a stone carving from Salisbury Cathedral. Dig a bit deeper, and you'll find that the town was originally named after William Salisbury, an eighteenth-century settler notorious for tying his servant girl to a horse and dragging her along the ground to her death. Her misdeed—she had tried to flee.

Sentenced to death by hanging, Salisbury was saved by influential friends who had the sentence delayed until "he should be a hundred." By the century's end he had celebrated his hundredth birthday, and the court had lost interest, so the sentence was never imposed. Much later, in 1879, his great-granddaughter sanitized the story.

The town of Salisbury, comprising the villages of Salisbury and Lakeville and several hamlets, is part of the cluster of small, overwhelmingly white communities—lily white—collectively called Connecticut's northwest corner. They sit in Litchfield County, which Mildred Savage—a Connecticut author with a keen social conscience—described as a "ragged-edge square on the map," but which, in fact, is oblong. Far from the homogenous suburbs and heaving multiracial cities linked by highways, and set off from the rest of the county by the Litchfield Hills, the northwest corner prizes itself for its quaint town centers and picturesque landscapes. Stippled with lakes and streams, the land is lush and sleek. Cows graze alongside winding country lanes, like Hammertown Road, one of the prettiest roads I've ever seen, where I used to jog.

Many areas still have their village green, a relic of the era when residents assembled to discuss local affairs. But the community spirit promised by those village greens is merely an illusion of a long-lost past—if, indeed, it ever existed.

If you go further back in history, long before those New Englanders built their stone walls, you'll discover that the area was called Weataug—"Wigwam place"—after the village-dwelling Weataug people, who lived by farming, hunting and fishing, and were part of the Algonquin-speaking Mohican nation.

The year 1676 marked the first known contact between the Weataug and the Europeans trekking across the land. Reverend Joseph Crossman's 1803 *New-Year's Discourse* notes that the Weataug, whose main village boasted seventy wigwams, were "friendly and hospitable Indians, especially to the whites, and encouraged their settlement." Indeed, in 1721 two settlers purchased land comprising more than half of present-day Salisbury. Another large land sale took place in 1729; the Weataug remained in a reserved area alongside their main village. In 1742—four years after the area was renamed Salisbury and one year after the new town was incorporated—the *Report of a Committee respecting the Lands of the Sharon and Salisbury Indians* suggested that the Weataug didn't understand the sale terms and thought they could still live there. To keep the peace, it was recommended that some be allowed to stay. A 1774 Litchfield County census listed thirty-five Native Americans living in Salisbury, their history largely forgotten—at least by the whites.

By the nineteenth century Salisbury was a hub of the early iron industry, teeming with Irish immigrants who forged iron on nearby Mt Riga. Their working-class descendants became known as "raggies." Religious and class tensions were never far from the surface.

In 1882 St Mary's Catholic Church in Lakeville erected a twelve-foot cross on its lawn bearing a life size replica of a bloody Jesus. Repulsed by this ostentatious display, the town's Protestant ladies threatened to replace their Irish Catholic housekeepers with, "Colored servant girls from New-York, or if necessary, from the South," according to the *New York Times*. The cross was removed; the portended African-Americans never arrived.

Fifteen years later those Protestant ladies and their daughters must've balked at the *Evening Register*'s report of "swarthy sons of Italy" bringing their Catholic traditions to Litchfield County. But these immigrants settled in Canaan and Torrington. In the first half of the twentieth century, Russian Jews fleeing persecution settled in nearby Sharon. Their children weren't welcome at the high school, so many of them moved to adjacent Amenia, New York. One family settled in Lakeville; vandals damaged their home and left a sign: "Go home Jews."

Salisbury village boasts an exceptionally pretty main street. Approaching Main Street from the south, the stone library is on the right followed by the pristine white Congregational Church. Across Main Street is the white town hall, artfully designed to harmonize with the nineteenth-century architecture. Past an array of tasteful shops and the brick St John's Episcopal Church, at the other end of the street, where the road divides, stands the imposing White Hart Inn. Its front lawn once boasted an impressive pine tree—proudly decorated each December when the village looks like a Christmas card.

However, one morning residents awoke to find their cherished tree chopped down and lying corpse-like across the manicured lawn—an anonymous gesture of defiance against the haves. More ominously, according to Arthur Herzog's *A Murder in Our Town*, between March 1978 and October 1985, when the original town hall was burnt down, the town had twenty-two suspicious fires—the probable cause arson. This was more than any other Connecticut–New York–Massachusetts Tri-State community. To Herzog, the events signaled "Salisbury's curious denial of reality" about the long-simmering resentment towards the well-to-do. Most culprits were never caught.

Today the town's immigrants are mostly wealthy New Yorkers and occasional film stars. Like other northwest corner towns, Salisbury has been hollowed out by the stealthy hike in property prices. As the young left, New York City weekenders bought up local homes. Many weekenders and wealthy people hiding behind their gates have little interest in local affairs, aside from bemoaning the scarcity of local help.

But when my parents first happened upon Salisbury, they'd been seduced by its illusion of unspoiled, idyllic small-town America. There, on the Massachusetts border of northwest Connecticut, they'd built their dream home on thirteen and one-half wooded acres, just a twelve-minute drive past Salisbury village.

• • •

"It's too long."

I'm thirteen, standing in front of the full-length mirror with Daddy sitting on the floor, legs crossed, pins in his mouth, measuring the skirt length from the floor up and sticking in pins in preparation for hemming.

"How about there?"

"Another inch"

"Let's try a half."

"Okay."

"Stop fidgeting. Stand up straight."

"I am straight," I say, adjusting my hip.

"Okay, turn."

I turn.

It's December. Daddy's making Bettina and me ivy green faux fur dirndl skirts with sky blue silky lining trimmed at the bottom with tiny gold bells that tinkle when we walk. We will wear them on Christmas Day with pale blue blouses, and when we cross our legs, the lining will show, revealing the bells.

Daddy designed women's sportswear. Slim build, average height, brown hair, blue eyes and an oval face, he made his name in the 1950s and '60s, winning the 1958 Mortimer C. Ritter Award—the fashion industry's Oscar—for outstanding achievement for his designs and his impact on the industry. He was College Town's chief designer.

"College girls are very basic," he told the *New York Herald Tribune* in his Southern drawl. "You have to creep up on them, be stylish without their ever knowing anything about it."

One of eight children, Daddy was born almost a year before the United States entered World War One and grew up in the small rural town of Rockmart, Georgia, fifty miles northwest of Atlanta. The Drews had a farm with cotton, beans, chickens and cows. Daddy had to get up early to milk the cows before school. He often walked to school barefoot and always missed the first week because he had to pick cotton.

His love of sewing began while sitting on his mama's lap and watching her quilt. Aged five, he asked her for a square to quilt and proved so adept he was soon sewing clothes for his sisters' dolls. After graduating from Rockmart High School, he began working at the textile mill, and when young art teacher Velma Wilder moved to Rockmart, he became one of her first students. Recognizing his talent, she encouraged him to continue his art studies. He was already mesmerized by the world of fashion. The Great Depression made new clothes a dream for most Americans, but Hollywood's Metro-Goldwyn-Meyer films brought high fashion to small towns, presenting couturier Gilbert Adrian's creations under the credit "Gowns by Adrian."

Daddy saved his money and moved to Baltimore to enroll at the Maryland Institute of Art. He graduated with a Diploma then enrolled in the United States Army, which sent him to the Philippines and the Solomon Islands. A charmer, he made friends easily: we have a very fine water color portrait of him in army garb painted by a Filipino. The army then moved him to Japan as part of the American occupation. Following his discharge Daddy settled in New York City to study at the newly-founded Fashion Institute of Technology, graduating in 1949.

After the war, the mass production of fabrics and clothing made fashion more affordable. Designers like Daddy were sent to Paris to adapt *haute couture* for the burgeoning American consumer market. He designed for Country Set, Dalton of America, Jonathan Logan, Ilene Ricky, Toby Tanner and Vera, often with his own label. He introduced the "union suit" to be worn under shorts—forerunner of the body suit, and promoted elegant jump suits for easy home entertaining. He designed TWA's wardrobe for flight attendants and ground staff, complete with mini-skirts, jaunty coats and flowing neck scarves for chilly weather.

But the fashion world is cut-throat, and the market's vicissitudes meant never-ending competition. Daddy's career began declining, he once confided, when my parents joined the great white middle-class drift to the suburbs, moving to leafy Larchmont, New York, just a thirty-minute train ride to Manhattan but a cultural wasteland shaped around conformity. After twenty-two years designing women's sportswear, Daddy became acting curator, then curator of costumes at the Fashion Institute of Technology's Design Laboratory, also teaching evening classes.

He loved the work. Visitors to the Design Lab sent him warm letters of appreciation, and students responded with enthusiastic teaching evaluations and wonderful gifts—a large sterling silver thimble engraved with his name and a wooden plaque commemorating his great teaching.

Mommy, too, had her dreams. As a child in Atlanta she had won a newspaper-publicized contest to draw the best Easter rabbit. Later she attended Atlanta's High Museum and School of Art, then moved to New York City in 1946, where she joined the Art Students League, studied with abstract expressionist painter James Brooks and did color work with Hans Hoffman. But needing to earn her living, she turned to the fashion industry. She became a coordinator for a velvet fabric house, tasked with convincing top designers to include a velvet dress, suit or coat in their collections. She would show up in a velvet suit, or sporting velvet gloves and beret; her soft Southern accent, she soon realized, was an asset. The volume dress manufacturers followed the lead of the top designers, launching the "velvet trend." While she was still Alyce Byrnes, the journalist Jean Rooney wrote a feature on her for the *Atlanta Constitution*. The article includes a photo of her sitting in her Greenwich Village studio apartment, with three of her oils on the wall behind her. Auburn-haired, blue-eyed, she is beautiful, dream-like, serious-looking. One hand holds a magazine; the other, nails polished, flutters, almost off the page.

My parents married in 1951 and within five years had two children. Mommy wanted to resume working when Bettina was six months old so hired our babysitter—a mature woman—to work as a nanny. But the evening before Mommy was due to start her new job, she and Daddy went out. Later that night Bettina began crying and wouldn't stop. When Mommy undressed her the next morning, she discovered that the babysitter had put on her booties with rubber bands, preventing the blood from circulating to her feet, which had turned black. Bettina quickly recovered, but Mommy called up her new employer and quit that same morning, to remain a full-time mother.

It tore at her, but she became accustomed to the status of upper-middle-class housewife, especially when they moved to Larchmont where, in the 1960s, it wasn't acceptable for women to work outside the home. She sat up her easel in the basement—Daddy had a small workroom off the kitchen, where he sketched on Sundays. She joined the Mamaroneck Artists' Guild, exhibited at the local Art Barn, earned a State adult teaching certificate in Interior Design and became an interior designer at the prestigious W & J Sloane, the country's first home furnishings store.

Mommy hadn't wanted to retire when Daddy did—her career was at its peak. But she acquiesced, setting up a studio in a spare bedroom and dedicating herself to painting, despite her illness. In the two creative years that they shared in Salisbury, they were happy.

And when I first saw the house, years before I moved to England, I was smitten.

CHAPTER 4

My relationship with England developed by chance. As a child I had been mightily impressed by fairy tales of wild boars hunting truffles in haunted northern forests. In the late 1980s I began stopping off in England *en route* to South Africa, where I was doing doctoral research on socialists in the national liberation struggle.

I loved London's multicultural vibrancy, but the English were a mystery to me. I could never comprehend how Inspector Morse—hero of the Oxford-based detective show—knew which characters were secretly in love—I saw no obvious signs. One day I finally grasped that the answer lay not in their words, but in their silences. The English have codified their unspoken words into a language I've never understood—easier to learn French. Not understanding and fearing to be misconstrued, I suppressed my natural spontaneity.

Much later I began writing a biography of Oxford-educated Sidney Bunting, a British-born idealist seeking the socialist utopia only to be persecuted by the Communist International and expelled by the Communist Party of South Africa he had helped found in 1921. A visiting fellowship at Magdalen College, Oxford, which Bunting had attended, allowed me to drink in the culture that shaped him. But I was nonetheless an outsider.

In 1992 I fell in love with an Englishman named Jack, and in 1995 we moved to York, where I began teaching African politics at the University of York. I had lived in South Africa during a tumultuous surge of the anti-apartheid struggle and, again, during the democratic transition. Exuberant but emotionally grueling and often excruciatingly lonely years. I was so happy to be settled.

I adored Jack. One weekend we hired bikes with his young daughter to ride on a country lane. I had only learned to ride when I was eighteen and never got over my fear of falling, so I couldn't go far. But his daughter set off smoothly, and Jack shot off, his big body hanging over the too-small bike frame, his face lit with that uninhibited childlike joy so rare in an adult.

We hoped to have a baby and talked about it often. But ever capricious, nature let me down: drop by drop, month by month, my fertility ebbed away. It was a great sorrow, and for a long time I was very sad. But I accommodated myself, throwing myself into trade union and volunteer activities and, of course, my research and teaching. Every so often, though, I think longingly, lovingly of that little baby I never had, then tenderly tuck the thought back where it belongs, in the deep recesses of my mind.

Someone once told me there are three responses to shock: fight, flight and freeze. Almost invariably, I freeze. Only later, when I've had a chance to ponder the situation, do I flee, and only rarely do I fight. As with most of our personality traits, this behavior is undoubtedly rooted in childhood, but it's been reinforced by my years in England.

Jack was magical, but unpredictable. One warm Saturday evening when we had been together five years, I hummed to myself as I set the table in our garden, full of quiet happiness. We sat down, and I passed Jack the salad.

"I've rented a flat, and I'm moving out Monday morning," he announced.

I sat in silence, unable to find words to express the emotions flooding through me. I had had no idea he was unhappy. After dinner we followed our Saturday evening routine and strolled to the pub. But I was still unable to process my feelings into words. Only Monday after he had left did I press my face into the bathrobe he had left behind and sob. A week later, I penned a letter professing my love and begging him to return, sent care of one of his friends, and some months later he did.

For comfort while he was gone I adopted a six-week-old long-haired black kitten with olive eyes whom I named Margo. A shy creature, for those first months I was her only human contact, and she embraced me as her mother. When to my joy Jack finally reappeared, she took one look up at the large, loud, looming being and fled, through his legs and up two flights of stairs. I found her quivering behind a dresser. But she soon became attached to him.

• • •

Periodically I visited Daddy, taking my laptop so that I could write—my office, Mommy's painting studio, now a bedroom; my desk, the one on which Daddy had sketched his fashion designs. I would type up the notes I gathered from archives and interviews and spread the printed pages on the floor to form a large square, normally five pages wide and five down—my normal working mode. Kneeling over them, I would look for connections and patterns, cutting the pages and shifting them around to make a logical sequence. When I needed a break, I would scavenge in the attic, seeking secrets and mementos of the past, concealed, misplaced or forgotten. Then, having satisfied my urge to browse, I would return to my papers.

"Wow!" Daddy gasped when he first saw me sifting through Bunting's life on my knees. Bettina visited that summer. She had published a biography of American novelist Nelson Algren and acceded to my plea to read my Bunting chapters. Lounging on the back patio, she filled the margins with question marks and scrawled comments that I eagerly assimilated.

For some years Daddy dated a woman who called me "dear" and whose family was in the Social Register. Daddy said she had criticized her former husband for not earning enough money, although perhaps she was simply upset the marriage hadn't worked out. However, she dropped Daddy when his hearing declined, and her social circle, taking the cue, shunned him too.

One day, when he was 87, hard of hearing but otherwise fit, we were driving on Hammertown Road, and he mentioned a 92-year-old whom he was driving to church.

"I don't know what'll happen to me when I can't drive. Will anyone help me?"

It was a rare admission that he sensed the lack of community in a town with no public transportation and where the elderly who can't drive or get lifts are dubbed shut-ins. However, with the help of his pastor, I later found someone to drive him to church.

And as always, before I left for England he would remind me that when his time came, he wanted Mommy's and Bootsie's ashes draped across his shoulders before he was buried.

Daddy started becoming forgetful.

Bettina noticed and told his GP, Dr Peter Gott.

I found Dr Gott inept, but he had the virtue of making house calls in an area with relatively few doctors—some of whom surpassed him in incompetence. And he was famed for his syndicated medical column, "Ask Dr Gott"—America's most widely-read. He even featured in a 1989 Oprah Winfrey show concerned with "demystifying the 'God' image of doctors"—quite the New England dandy in a polka-dot bow tie and tweed jacket—revealing one of his own medical errors.

Bettina eventually took Daddy to a neurologist, who diagnosed him with memory loss and prescribed pills. Soon after, Daddy phoned Bettina, back in Missouri, and said he didn't feel well. Bettina called the visiting nurses. A nurse popped by Daddy's, then phoned Bettina to say she would drive him to Sharon Hospital for a check-up. Instead, she called an ambulance and left. By the time the ambulance men arrived, Daddy was out gardening. The men ignored his insistence he was fine—he was "pretty good for a dementia-type" one of them reported.

"They grabbed me and wrapped and tied me and drove me to the hospital," Daddy later confided.

Daddy spent an unnecessary night in the newly-privatized hospital, obliged to wait until the next day when his pastor could drive him home. But when Bettina called that morning, she was transferred to Dr Laurence Schweitzer, director of the hospital's Senior Behavioral Unit. They argued. Dr Schweitzer then instructed Daddy be confined against his will in the extremely high-priced Senior Behavioral Unit with no family contact for 72 hours. By then Daddy was already dressed and waiting in his room for the pastor. When hospital staff came to intern Daddy, he ran. They ran faster.

Bettina called me.

I called the unit holding him and introduced myself to the nurse.

"Your daughter's on the phone, and if you aren't nice, I won't let you speak to her," she told Daddy.

"You let me speak to my daughter!"

"Put my father on the phone, nurse!"

"Daddy, don't let them give you any injections."

"Don't you worry, darlin'. I won't."

Later, trying to understand the events, I would phone Dr Schweitzer to ask why he had ordered Daddy's internment. His response—"you're so duplicitous"—cut off our brief conversation. We had never spoken, and his words and unctuous tone made my blood run cold.

I would then discover that Dr Schweitzer had seen Daddy the year before, at Dr Gott's request, and diagnosed his dementia; I found an unfilled prescription for memory pills. However, according to Daddy's medical records, Dr Schweitzer never informed Dr Gott, nor had Dr Gott followed up. It's hardly surprising that someone with dementia might forget to fill a prescription. What is surprising is that the two doctors concerned "forgot" to confer with each other about their patient. I also learned that Dr Schweitzer had been dismissed from a Veteran's Administration hospital for alleged irregularities in the manner in which he prescribed medications. He vigorously denied the claim, but his defamation suit against the Department of Veterans Affairs was dismissed.

Just as twenty years earlier Mommy's GP had prevailed upon other GPs not to examine her, Dr Schweitzer had persuaded two other doctors to support Daddy's detention. Daddy's medical records show that one was the neurologist who'd just diagnosed him with mild dementia and knew full well he didn't need confinement, and the other, a GP whose report stressed that Daddy was wearing bedroom slippers. Of course, Daddy was wearing slippers. He had been picked up at home and often wore his ankle-high slippers out gardening as a protection against deer ticks.

Wearing slippers at home is not a sign of dementia.

Bettina rescued Daddy from the hospital. I flew over from England, and we went to meet the visiting nurses, at their request. In the meeting room we were seated opposite three very large women who stared fixedly at us across the table.

"Your father has dementia. He needs 24/7 nursing care," Nurse One began.

"That's not true," I replied. "People with mild to moderate dementia often live by themselves. They just need support."

"He's not driving, is he? You're not letting him drive?" Nurse Two leaned forward, her hefty bosom resting on the table.

"The research says people with mild to moderate dementia *can* drive safely," I countered. "It depends on the person. My father's driving is fine."

They pushed their services. I caught Bettina's eye.

"Well, you've certainly given us a lot to think about," she said, rising.

Daddy's attorney recommended he be examined by an out-of-state specialist—a precaution, I surmised, against small-town intrigues. Bettina, Daddy and I drove to New York University Medical Center in Manhattan. Daddy was looking especially snappy that day, in a suit and tie with red suspenders.

"Who dressed him?" a neurologist asked.

"He dressed himself."

The doctor's eyes widened in surprise, his preconceptions shaken.

Later, after Bettina returned to Missouri, I drove to the Salisbury Town Hall and met a woman from Elderly Services, middle-aged, smiling and attractive in her smart bob haircut.

"I'm glad you stopped by, Allison," she said eagerly. "I was hoping to speak to your father about elderly services." We chatted and agreed she would come by the next day at 10 am.

"He's just been diagnosed with dementia." My voice quivered.

The next morning Daddy and I got dressed up for our Town Hall visitor, Daddy in a suit and tie. We waited: 10:10, 10:15, 10:20; Daddy became impatient.

"Allison, I have to mow the lawn. I want to change."

"Daddy, hold on, I'll call the woman."

I zipped upstairs and sat at my desk, dialing several times with no answer. I finally reached her at 10:30. Her tone was frosty.

"I just got out of a meeting."

"But I thought you were coming at 10. We've been waiting for you."

"I can't come; I have another meeting."

"I thought we were going to discuss elderly services for my father."

"There are no elderly services."

"But what about the Friendly Visitors? You mentioned them yesterday. I would really like someone to stop by once a week and chat with him."

"Oh yes, you can call them and see if they'll come."

She hung up. I was stunned by her about-face.

"It's okay, Daddy," I called out. "She can't come. You can change." I left message after message for the Friendly Visitors. No one ever called back.

The following day, on the doorstep, I found a visiting card from a Torrington social worker who'd been given an anonymous tip that an elderly man with dementia was living on his own.

I duly called him.

He arrived promptly the next morning.

He was pleasant enough, petting Daddy's cat and talking about his own. He asked Daddy a series of questions, starting with his age.

Daddy couldn't remember if he was 88 or 89.

"Who is our President?"

"Oh … what's his name? I voted for his Daddy." Well, he identified him, even if he couldn't recollect his name.

"It's George W. Bush," I said.

Daddy nodded.

"And the governor's name?" asked the social worker.

I snorted—couldn't help it—and pointed out that I couldn't answer that one.

"You don't live here," countered the social worker.

"I study politics. I should know. My father doesn't need to."

The discussion over, the social worker rose.

"If I hear any more reports, we'll take his home and put him in an institution," he said as I walked him to his car.

I felt his threats had nothing to do with Daddy's well-being but with seizing an asset: I had read horror stories of states accumulating wealth by seizing private assets.

I was terrified.

Notwithstanding the trauma of the internment, Daddy was keen to resume his volunteer activities. After Mommy's death, he had worked part-time at the wonderful *Connecticut Yankee* clothing shop on Salisbury's Main Street, assisting customers and designing its ads for the *Lakeville Journal*. He had also volunteered at the hospital, the church, the town hall and historic sites, such as the Holley-Williams House.

Now, Thursday was his volunteering day. Mornings he staffed the reception desk at the Hotchkiss School's Tremaine Art Gallery. Founded in 1891 as a boarding school for boys aiming for Yale but now coed, the Hotchkiss School is the jewel in Salisbury's crown. It sits on 827 acres of fields, farmland and woods in Lakeville, on the road to Sharon. Its manicured grounds boast an array of red-brick buildings designed by leading architects and a trio of bronze bulls lounging on the lawn. Daddy loved working there: the students knew him, and he relished the cafeteria's lively atmosphere and the free lunch he got after his shift.

Afternoons he worked in the Posh Department at the Bargain Barn, an upmarket charity shop in nearby Sharon. The Thursday after Daddy's detention, I was browsing through a rack of Posh Department dresses while Daddy finished writing up a receipt for a solitary customer who went to pay the cashier in the main room. Suddenly Daddy collapsed sobbing on a stool behind the counter, his head bowed, his right hand over his eyes.

"What's wrong?" I rushed over to him, kneeling down.

"The hospital, those people, nothing, nothing ... I'm okay." He wiped away his tears.

The next day, sitting at his kitchen table, he took out a notepad and began writing to his close friend Larimore. Slim and elegant, Larimore had arrived in New York City in the 1970s to pursue her passion for the arts. With an introduction from Daddy's brother Raymond, she had become good friends with my parents.

"I want to tell her what happened."

But he couldn't get past the first line.

"I'll help you." I pulled a chair close and sat beside him.

"No, it's too painful. Sometimes … sometimes you don't want to remember." He put the letter aside and never finished it.

I had bought a skirt at the Bargain Barn and asked Daddy to help me set up the sewing machine so that I could hem it.

"Leave it on the dining room table."

"I wanted to wear it tomorrow."

"Leave it there."

"I'll do it if you help me set up the machine."

"Leave it."

The next morning, going to eat breakfast, I glanced at the dining room table. There was the skirt, neatly spread out, already hemmed with perfect, tiny stitches. Dr Schweitzer had claimed Daddy couldn't complete a simple sewing exercise. It seemed he had lied to justify Daddy's internment and make a buck on an overpriced bed.

Leafing through the *New York Times* at the kitchen table one Sunday, Daddy tapped the paper with his finger.

"I'd like to see that."

It was an advertisement for a major Coco Chanel exhibition at the Metropolitan Museum of Art.

"Let's go! Would Larimore be interested?"

"Why not? Call her."

The three of us met at the museum the following week. It was a great exhibit, a glorious day. We took photos of each other on the museum's rooftop; Larimore took one of me and Daddy, me in an olive green sweater, he in a white shirt and tie, one arm around me, the other holding his jacket.

Shunned by the town's Elderly Services, we proceeded on our own, enrolling Daddy in Meals on Wheels and the Veterans Administration medical system and hiring a part-time senior companion, who came five afternoons a week. I spent the summer there, when the lawn, the garden, the chopping of wood took most of Daddy's time. One day, as he and I sat at the kitchen table, he sketched a plan for a patio he had built near the stream. He wanted to gravel the paths and landscape with new plants. We went together to pick up the gravel.

"Now, let me talk," he said pointedly when we approached the man at the gravel pit. I did so, and together we got the gravel and revamped the patio.

I felt like a soccer mom accompanying her kid to his activities. Not only the Thursday volunteering. Mondays we went grocery shopping, and Fridays we drove to the Salisbury/Sharon Transfer Station—the town dump—where Daddy took his trash for recycling. The transfer station has a room called the swap shop where people drop off goods they no longer want but that others might find useful. No records are kept. People simply leave their used items on a long table or against a wall. I liked to browse through the used books and bric-a-brac and once found a coffee maker for Bettina.

Although more dependent, Daddy still sometimes slipped back into old habits.

Once, back late after eating out with a friend, I crept stealthily up the stairs.

"Allison! Where were you?" I turned and looked up. Daddy was on the landing in his underwear.

"I told you. I was having dinner with a friend."

"Till midnight?" He raised his wrist to look at the watch he never removed and, grumbling, went back to bed.

• • •

The town was far from ideal. But Daddy didn't want to move. He was completely at ease in nature. Aside from childhood recollections, landscapes—spatial relations—were his most deeply entrenched memories. A landmark person, when we went walking, he always spotted the bush marking our turning point. And when we drove, he always knew the route, even if he couldn't recall the street names.

Alongside his love of nature was his respect for its wildlife. One afternoon he and I strolled past the two white pillars towards Ravine Ridge Road to check his mail box on Route 41, his daily routine until his last year when it became too difficult.

A turtle, ten inches long, was crossing the drive.

"I need to move that turtle," I said.

"Leave it. It'll find its own way."

But I was worried about it. I wanted to put it in the foliage, away from the road. I picked it up. It panicked, its little legs flailing, its little paws frantically scratching the air. I managed to get the creature to the side of the road before putting it down, feeling sorry for its woes.

"I told you to leave it be," said Daddy.

CHAPTER 5

Christmas 2005. Daddy flew to Missouri to see Bettina, recovering from a broken leg, and occupied himself hanging her paintings. I went to Salisbury the first two weeks of January to take Daddy to his new Veterans Administration neurologist, who tested his memory with questions:

"What do doctors do?"

"Exactly what you're doing."

The neurologist and I exchanged glances. An unexpected answer, it was definitely correct.

The heavy snows drove the tiny field mice inside, where they took refuge in the insulated basement, the kitchen and the attic. In the eternal battle between mice and men, invariably the field mice won, and all we could do was contain them until they moved outdoors in the spring.

The snow meant Daddy couldn't work outside, so to keep busy he sewed a new pair of floor-length drapes, which his part-time senior companion helped him hang in the library.

"They give the room a new personality," he told me when I visited that summer.

As I sat typing at my desk, the phone rang.

It was the social worker.

"A woman from Salisbury Elderly Services called and said she'd just been out to see your father and found him on his own."

"So what? He's perfectly capable of staying in his house on his own. In any case, she's lying." I heard him gasp. "I'm here," I explained. "No one has come by." I drew a breath. "We're getting ready to go out. My father has to go to his jobs."

"*Jobs? Your father works?*"

"Yes, in an art gallery and a charity shop."

I never heard back from the social worker, but his call shattered my calm.

Daddy had fewer local friends but kept busy with his projects and occasional visits from out-of-state friends.

"I want to paint these urns and put geraniums in them," he told me one morning when we were out on the back porch. "I want you to pick up a can of white paint the next time you go out."

"Okay. The kitchen chairs need touching up, too."

Over the next few days, those hot, still summer days when time slows down, we sat outside working on the urns and the chairs, gazing periodically at the Berkshires and at a pair of wild turkeys strutting across the lawn with their chicks.

But beneath the tranquil surface, the senior companion was a problem. After I returned to York he canceled Daddy's doctor appointment against my instructions and was evasive with the Veterans Administration GP about his medications. I sensed he wanted Daddy to decline so that he could get more hours. I knew I had to replace him. And so I hired Matt.

• • •

Christmas 2006. Bettina and I visited Daddy. By then I had left Jack, taking Margo with me, although she returned to Jack's whenever I travelled. I still loved Jack, and in my heart I had longed to stay, but the love was no longer reciprocated—or so I felt. From the time he returned I was left out of every family holiday. There were no more Christmases with him, his mum and daughter. He wouldn't discuss it. Frozen in my own pain, I couldn't find the words to contest it. Reminded constantly of his rejection, I still hoped, the very morning I moved out, that he would ask me to stay. But he didn't. Was I wrong to leave him? Perhaps. Probably. I don't know. My head said leave, but my beating heart felt otherwise.

It was evening when I arrived in Salisbury. In the moonlight, Daddy's house sat snugly on the shimmering snow, the trees glittering with frost. On Christmas Day—our last with Daddy—Matt took photos of us sitting around the kitchen table, wearing comical spectacles and laughing. I accompanied Daddy to church. Main Street slick with ice, we stepped gingerly, arms linked.

"What's your hurry?" said Daddy. "Slow down. They won't shut us out."

Daddy had given up both his volunteer jobs. Julia, who worked at the Hotchkiss School, told me he couldn't even carry his lunch tray anymore—Matt brought it to him.

Pamela was due to start in January. She sent a Christmas card, and I could so easily have interviewed her and checked her references while I was there.

My second fateful error.

• • •

By spring 2007 Daddy was less steady on his feet, having fallen three times, in February, March and April. Matt told me about the falls and said he had instructed the part-time companions to be extra vigilant about following Daddy to make sure he got where he wanted to go. Knowing that people with dementia sometimes wander, I discussed this possibility with Matt, but he thought it unlikely because of Daddy's frailty and breathlessness and because the companions were expected to accompany him outside. By then Pamela was the main part-timer, as one of the women had changed jobs, and the other had moved further away. We agreed she would stay over on the alternate Saturday nights when Matt was in the city with his girlfriend. He seemed confident about her, and I felt happy and relieved after our conversation.

Larimore came up from Manhattan for a weekend in early June. Matt snapped photos of her and Daddy standing cheek to cheek, she in a black jacket, arms draped around him, he, in a shirt, tie and checked sweater, both beaming with gentle happiness. Matt wanted to take them to lunch after church. But Daddy insisted on his after-church routine—jeans, coffee and crossword—and refused, so they returned home. Bettina came later that month *en route* to Europe and met Pamela, who stopped by briefly.

"She seemed nice ... a bit hippyish," Bettina told me, adding, "Daddy's fine, but he's frailer and leans against the walls and furniture when he crosses a room." Julia confirmed this when Matt brought Daddy to visit the Hotchkiss School that June.

"He clung to my arm when we walked down the corridor; he just couldn't manage on his own anymore."

So did Daddy's pastor. After the church service, he would wait at the chapel door for Daddy, who'd pause and rest at each pew as he proceeded down the aisle.

In mid-July, Daddy's friend Jonathan saw him sitting alone in a car parked outside St Mary's Church. Daddy waved, and they chatted.

"He seemed fine," Jonathan would later tell me.

Bettina had planned to visit Daddy on her return from Europe, but she and Matt argued. Larimore had hoped to visit the weekend of July 21, but Matt told her it wouldn't be convenient.

Daddy had five friends from Massachusetts, Fran, Woody, Bob, John and Ray, whom he affectionately called "my boys." Every autumn for twenty-five years they hunted deer on his property with bows and arrows. They would arrive in the middle of the night, park in the driveway, cross the lawn to the woods, perch in trees and watch for deer. Sitting in the dark beneath a starry sky was the perfect place to be alone with your thoughts, Fran told me.

I hated the idea of hunting. When I was thirteen Daddy read me a passage from Marjorie Kinnan Rawling's novel, *The Yearling*, set in 1870s Florida. It concerned the boy Jody, forced to kill his beloved fawn Flag because it was eating the family's crops. His left hand holding the book, his right hand covering his eyes, Daddy began weeping, and I, too, read the novel and wept. But Daddy explained our deer had to be culled so that they didn't starve during the long snowy winters.

The hunters would come in at dawn for cups of hot coffee and *Thomas' English muffins* with butter and Daddy's home-made jam. Later they would drop off joints of venison, which Daddy put in his basement freezer. They even helped him build a footbridge across his stream, and Daddy mounted a plaque on the footbridge engraved to "my boys."

"Good times," Fran used to say.

Right off after Daddy vanished, Fran and Woody came to look for him. They climbed into trees to peer around and put on waders to search the stream under the Ravinehurst bridge and the swampy area northeast of Daddy's house. Beavers, a protected species, had dammed the stream under that bridge. Gradually, the surrounding area became very muddy, although still walkable in waders, and people called it a swamp. Experienced trackers who knew the property and surrounding areas like the back of their hands, Fran and Woody slogged deeper into the swamp than the other searchers, far beyond any tracks.

But they doubted Daddy had left on foot.

"In his physical condition how far could he have gone?" Woody pondered. "I just had to satisfy myself that we did not overlook anything. If anything dies in the swamp, say a deer or any animal, the turkey vultures are there circling overhead. There were no vultures."

No vultures.

A week or two after the disappearance, Woody came back on his own. I accompanied him as we traipsed through the woods, looking in every nook and cranny, even an old pipe. At one point, turning around, I panicked. Had I wandered and become lost? All I could see were trees for miles and miles. How could I ever find my way home? But Woody, like Daddy a landmark person, knew the wood's twists and turns and the way back.

• • •

The term *wandering*, when associated with dementia, is loosely bandied about. Since Daddy had dementia, he must have wandered off—that was the single line of enquiry pursued by the police, who did everything possible to present Daddy's disappearance as "normal."

Donna Algase, Professor Emerita at the University of Michigan Nursing School, defines "dementia wandering" as repetitive action manifested in lapping, pacing and random movements that is temporally disordered and spatially disoriented. Lapping means moving around in a circuit, whether regular or irregular; pacing means moving back and forth repeatedly; random means moving in a pattern that can't be easily classified, but that is neither lapping nor pacing. Some people with dementia display these patterns, but many don't—with no prior history of wandering, Daddy was in the latter category.

Jan Dewing, Sue Pembrey Chair of Nursing at Edinburgh's Queen Margaret University, reminds us that wandering is healthy for all of us, including those with dementia; it is the possible consequences of wandering—falling, getting lost—that are problems, not wandering itself. In fact, being locked up and forced to sit still is bad for our physical and mental health.

Indeed, wandering used to have positive and even romantic connotations. The tourist *wanders* around Europe to soak up its distinctive atmosphere. I began my work as a twentieth-century historian *wandering* in search of South Africa's socialist movement: I loved perusing its literature in the old British Library's domed reading room and, later, in the South African Library in Cape Town's delightful Company's Garden. My *wanderings* took me to England where I fell in love. During the anti-apartheid struggle I even published an article under the *nom de plume*, A. Zwerver, meaning *a wanderer*.

Any departure without a fixed destination or any journey that meanders *en route* to its final point can be deemed wandering. But wandering in association with dementia is pejorative. Ambling and rambling; dancing and prancing; hiking, hopping, loping and jogging; promenading and plodding; roaming and roving; sauntering, skipping, straying and strolling; traipsing and trudging and just plain walking. People with dementia are denied these varied forms of movement, caricatured by the term *wandering*, like zombies stripped of their individuality.

In Salisbury dementia is spoken about in hushed tones. The old are slipped quietly into expensive nursing homes, so that it's extremely rare to see a very elderly—let alone disabled—person on Main Street. It takes guts and careful planning for very elderly Salisbury residents to remain at home. The lack of public transport and dependence on cars means that walking is stigmatized—the only walkers are out-of-town hikers keen to try the Appalachian Trail.

The police often rely on neurological conditions to explain disappearances. I learned this several years after Daddy's disappearance, when I read Connecticut author Michael Dooling's book, *Clueless in New England*, an analysis of three unsolved missing persons cases, including that of ten-year-old Connie Smith, who vanished from Lakeville in July 1952. Although amnesia is rare, and seldom wipes out the entire memory, nonetheless a disproportionate number of missing persons cases are attributed to amnesia. Dooling points out that missing people are often described as being lost in the woods, as though in a fairytale. Similarly, disappearances of elderly people are frequently attributed to dementia and linked to the idea of wandering and becoming lost in the woods.

Certain individuals baldly told me that people with dementia should be institutionalized—as though incarceration is the answer to all social problems. And some doctors have suggested people with dementia should be denied the right to vote. But, asks an American Association of Retired Persons representative, "Why should your next-door neighbor be given a greater barrier to voting than you, just because they have a medical diagnosis?" Indeed, no American should be prevented from voting.

Dementia should be seen as a *challenge* not a problem. Society's stigmatization of the illness is the problem. The *World Alzheimer Report 2012* defines stigma as "an attribute, behaviour or reputation which is socially discrediting" and "causes an individual to be mentally classified by others in an undesirable, rejected stereotype."

People with dementia tirelessly challenge these stereotypes. In Britain, the Alzheimer's Society stresses that persons with dementia should "receive care and support that is based on individual need, rather than assumptions about the condition." Yet those with dementia are often excluded from discussions about their own care. The Alzheimer's Society underlines the need to assume that all adults can make their own decisions, unless it has been shown otherwise and "all practical steps to help them to make a decision have been taken without success."

Likewise, in the United States, the Alzheimer's Association highlights the need to ask individuals with dementia what they want. "They wish not to be defined by decline and limitations and had suggestions … for improving relationships, helping others understand how to communicate with a person with dementia and how to keep them engaged in the daily life of their communities." One person made a simple but telling appeal: "Treat us as normal people. We're still here, just a little slower and sometimes confused." Another person added: "I think my skills have developed over time, getting beyond the initial scare ... finding kindred friends, realizing that lost skills can be replaced—bolstered with others, that many of the outcomes of dementia can be embraced and enjoyed."

As I read the accounts of people stigmatized as a result of dementia—both those with the disease and their carers—I remembered the dismissive attitudes of the visiting nurses, and later, after Daddy's disappearance, of some townspeople. Daddy had been very able to express his views about his lifestyle and his care. Yet, to all appearances, he had been written off. And the stigma of dementia tarred not only Daddy but his family.

• • •

An employee of the local retirement community, Noble Horizons, claimed to have seen someone matching Daddy's description on the Monday after the disappearance. She said he had difficulties speaking, but that he had uttered the words "this is a loving home" and "lost." She described him as clean-shaven and wearing clean clothes.

"If he spent two nights outside, that's not possible," Detective Warren told me.

"But my father's whiskers were very slow growing. They were white; they didn't show up against his skin," I argued.

They'd searched Noble Horizons' grounds with canines, he replied.

The police used canines, low-flying planes, helicopters and infrared lights in the assumption that Daddy had left his house on foot. If Daddy had started up the conservation road that day, but turned back, too tired and breathless to continue, or if he had collapsed on the road and been found and removed, surely he would have left footprints and other traces. But aside from the scent, no footprints, trampled earth, broken twigs or other signs of human passage that day were seen. No vultures, no animal tracks, no signs of a human having been dragged away.

Not even a loose-fitting slip-on shoe.

CHAPTER 6

Some 750,000 people, on average, go missing each year in the United States; up to 100,000 cases are active on any particular day. Connecticut's *State Police Missing Persons Protocol* (January 2007) provided minimal guidelines for missing persons cases. The following year, the state published *Guidelines for Handling Missing Persons Investigations and Acceptance of Reports*, which incorporated detailed guidelines copied from the procedures of other states.

"Thoroughly search the immediate and surrounding area in a logical and systematic manner. 1) Process any potential crime scene for evidence. 2) Identify and interview potential witnesses."

Potential crime scene. There it was.

The last known location of a missing person should be processed as a potential crime scene both to find evidence and to eliminate the possibility of police preconceptions or bias.

• • •

I realized that first summer that, presumably inadvertently, the police ensured there was no evidence of foul play by failing to treat Daddy's home—his last known location—as a potential crime scene. Without having done so—in the absence of a body—it was virtually impossible to determine if a crime had been committed. But seeing no obvious signs of struggle, the police didn't process the house—although one of them later ticked the box indicating it had been processed.

They didn't check the caller ID, pill tray, garbage or bedroom sheets or test for blood. They didn't examine Matt's computer for emails, which might have helped with the time frame. According to the police records I received, they didn't check whether Pamela had a laptop or cell phone with her. They looked in Matt's car that first night; they wanted to check Pamela's trunk, but she said it was jammed.

"I can't open it. They key goes in it, and it doesn't open. The lock device is broken," she told them. So they let her leave without checking.

Nor, according to the police records, did they request credit card or sales receipts from the three individuals present that evening, Pamela, Matt and Anna, or separate them and ask them each to write witness statements.

Only Matt gave a written statement. His account read:

"At around 3:00 pm I left the residence and picked up my girlfriend ... so we could spend the day together. When I left [Pamela] and Thomas were watching TV together. [Anna] and I returned to the residence at around 7.30 pm."

Why did Matt refer to "spending the day" with his girlfriend when he was picking her up late in the afternoon?

The police didn't clarify this or verify his statement, either by interviewing Anna, checking train times for the Wassaic, New York Metro-North Train Station or accessing credit card receipts.

Trooper Grant spoke to Pamela that first evening, reporting that she "observed Thomas walk out of the back door of the residence." Detective Warren's application to obtain Daddy's phone records likewise stated: "[Pamela] told Trooper [Grant] that about 7:20 pm Drew walked out the back door of the residence." Yet an interview with Pamela the next day reported that she "hadn't actually 'seen him' walk out."

The Sunday after the disappearance, the police learned that Pamela was at her brother's house in Falls Village, so two troopers drove there to inspect her car. Pamela's town clerk sister Susan, hovering nearby, told them Pamela was out on an errand, so they left.

"The cops wanted to look in her trunk, but it doesn't open because it has been jammed for a week," Susan told her family. "Pamela suggested to the police they make a campfire and a drumming circle."

Troopers returned that afternoon.

"Pamela is on Craig's front porch right now giving a statement to other police ... Time is now 3 PM Sunday," Susan reported.

Pamela told the police she had arrived at Daddy's house at 9:30 am the day before.

"In the morning, Matt pretty much stayed to himself upstairs and around the house," she said. "I stayed with Tom and we spent 45 minutes or so out on the patio in the sun. Tom was alert and happy. At about 12:30 pm I prepared lunch for Tom and served it to him in the kitchen."

Did Pamela remember Daddy's sister Mildred's call? Perhaps the police didn't know about it yet; they didn't ask. Pamela continued:

"During the afternoon, Tom and I spent some more time out on the patio. Tom was trimming the hedges and seemed to really be enjoying himself. At around 6:15 pm, I prepared Tom's evening meal."

Providing little detail about what Daddy did that day, Pamela offered detailed descriptions of the Meals on Wheels food he allegedly ate. But her claims about food couldn't be verified since the police never looked through the trash.

Later they watched TV.

"Tom was not very interested in the movie and after about 10 or 15 minutes he got up and said, 'I've got to get going' … Tom put on a *light tan jacket (maybe brown or white)* and left the living room while I continued to watch the movie. About 5 minutes later I got up to check on Tom and found the front door was locked." She then explained:

"Normally, when Tom and I went outside we would go through the garage or front door because the steps were a lot easier. I figured he must have changed his mind and was upstairs using the bathroom. A few minutes later when I didn't see or hear him I went upstairs to check. I couldn't find Tom anywhere upstairs and called to him but got no answer."

• • •

One week missing

That Sunday I went to the light-filled Congregational Church, which Daddy attended. I was seeking people who'd listen to my concerns. Yet so eager were people to accept Pamela's claim, that when the pastor saw me, he asked the congregation to pray for Tom Drew, who'd "wandered away." I sat stunned, immovable.

We don't know he walked away, I thought. *He could have been driven away*. Aside from the scent the canines picked up, there were no other signs that he had walked up the conservation road that Saturday—and if he had, how could walking up a straight road be construed as wandering? Nor had any canine picked up his scent on a vehicle road. I had come to say those very words, but other words had been voiced before I could speak, and I sat there, mute.

During the week I met Detective Warren at Troop B barracks in North Canaan—known locally as Canaan. With important limestone and marble quarries, Canaan had once been a busy railroad junction, but its rail passenger service stopped in 1971, and its Union Railroad Station was destroyed in a 2001 arson attack. Nowadays it's a declining blue collar town with an Italian and Catholic tradition and a faded but appealing main street. It was the first time I had visited the barracks, a squat, two-story red-brick 1940s building. Before World War Two State Police Station B had been located on West Main Street in the town center. But the state police expanded significantly in the 1940s, so the station was moved out to Route 7, near the Massachusetts border—a rusty neon State Police sign and an old-fashioned car out front mementos of bygone days.

The detective showed me to a room with a table, let me go through the files and, after checking with his superior, kindly made copies of the documents I selected, which included Daddy's phone records for the week up to July 22. I felt he wanted to be helpful. But he never applied for Matt's internet record for July 20-21, which was accessed through Daddy's phone line.

The Friday, July 20 phone records showed three calls between Daddy's house and Matt's girlfriend, two from Anna, at 4:30 pm for 3.34 minutes, and 4:35 pm for 8.04 minutes, and one outgoing call—presumably Matt—at 4:53 for 2.08 minutes. Then, at 5:35 pm a 16-minute call from Bridgeport, Connecticut. Daddy knew no one from Bridgeport and could scarcely have maintained a 16-minute conversation. The police could have traced the number's ownership and checked whether the owner knew Matt or Pamela, but they didn't. After the Bridgeport call came Bettina's 4.06 minute call at 6:06 pm, the last call that evening. Other nights that week, Matt and Anna had called each other around ten. Was Matt even at Daddy's house on Friday night, I reflected? Could Pamela have come over?

The Saturday, July 21 records listed a 12:03 pm call from Mildred for 7.39 minutes. They showed a 3.01 minute call to Pamela's in-laws at 10:02 am, a 9.19 minute call to middle-aged Lakeville couple Ron and Ronnie at 11:34 am, and calls to Pamela's home at 1:17 pm for 3.49 minutes and to her in-laws at 1:22 for 2.25 minutes. They also showed three brief calls to Pamela's neighbors between 4:15 and 4:17 pm. Very few outgoing calls compared to the previous Saturday when Pamela had spent almost ninety minutes on the phone to various family members. Although she told the police she was at the house, wide awake, the entire day, couldn't she have left part of that day? The detective checked a few Saturday afternoon calls; the police files I would receive over the years indicated no further checking.

I called Aunt Mildred and asked her whom she spoke to.

"A woman answered and said Tom's sleeping on the patio, and Matt's getting ready to go out," Mildred said. "'Don't bother waking him, I'll call later,' I told her. But I got involved in something and forgot to call back."

"Can't you phone Mildred and interview her?" I asked Detective Warren. "Can't you use her claim to question Matt about when he left?"

Instead, Mildred called the detective to ask how the search was going. Told that her brother had left on foot, she had no reason to doubt the police—no one wanted to consider foul play. Besides, Mildred was crazy about Matt, and he was very fond of her, he confided to me. He didn't have much family, so Mildred had become a surrogate aunt to him. For her part, she wouldn't countenance any questioning of his account.

"You know how fond he was of your Daddy," she chided me.

Nor did the police verify the 11:34 am call to Ron and his wife Ronnie, who was friends with Matt. Ronnie volunteered with Daddy, talking his ear off, oblivious to his poor hearing. Her words meandered like those of the mouse's tale in *Alice in Wonderland*; Daddy and I would catch each other's eyes, smiling, because it was impossible to follow her. Shortly after the disappearance she broke off contact with Matt and stopped volunteering, saying it reminded her of Daddy. I've speculated whether Matt phoned Ronnie and left Daddy's house around noon to visit her, telling a white lie because he didn't want his girlfriend to know. Or maybe Ronnie was smoking a joint, and he didn't want the cops to know. Or maybe it wasn't Matt who called. Several years later, Bettina would ask Ronnie about the call.

"It must have been Matt," she replied, gazing into space. Perhaps he had called to thank her for a Friday night music group at her house, she suggested. The police never checked at the time, so we'll never know for sure.

People preferred to blame the victim. I had lunch with Jocelyn, a teacher with an artistic eye and a flair for flamboyant colors who'd been fond of Daddy.

"The police haven't found him because he crossed a stream, and the dogs lost his scent," she insisted—a ludicrous claim. She mentioned Pamela.

"She's an odd bird."

"Why do you say that?" My stomach knotted.

"She called me at home right after Matt hired her. She wanted to know about your dad. I told her he was a charming elderly gentleman."

"But why did you call her an odd bird?"

"I thought she was aggressive. There was a boundary issue. I scarcely knew her, but she called me at home. There was something off."

"But if you thought that, why didn't you tell us before she started working for us?"

"I knew she was odd, but I didn't know she was that odd. In any case, it would have been worse if it had been a child who disappeared."

All human beings are equally important, I longed to say. *They must be found, no matter who they are.* But I couldn't speak.

Often I encountered silence. After lunch I went to the bank. The cashier stared at my check, then sidled up to a colleague, check face up in her hands, and nudged her. The colleague glanced at the check and nodded.

The teller returned, gave me my money, and I left.

Yet there were small kindnesses. Daddy's pastor dropped by, a woman who lived at Noble Horizons called to offer sympathy and a Windsor woman sent me a lovely card. Desperate for the slightest gesture of support, I wrote back; her church organized a prayer circle for Daddy. But I never heard from Daddy's former girlfriend or her circle.

• • •

We had a lead!

A Taconic Road resident told the police he had been watching TV on the Saturday evening. Sometime between 7 pm and 8:30, he had seen an elderly man walking south on the road in front of his house, about 100 feet away. The old man "was walking slowly kind of humped over obviously with a definite problem … The man was wearing a maroon shirt or sweatshirt with possible khaki pants or light brown pants"—no jacket. "This man's head was definitely looking down on the road not left or right and he wasn't walking fast but he didn't walk with a shuffle."

A similar sighting was reported around the corner, on Hammertown Road. Around 6:30 or 7 pm, a woman had seen an old man, "shuffling at a decent pace and looking down." He was wearing "khaki pants, white t-shirt with a sweater around his waist walking west."

He turned around in front of her house and walked east towards Taconic Road. Matt had said Daddy was wearing a maroon sweatshirt and jeans that day. Could Daddy have been wearing khaki pants or were the witnesses mistaken about the color?

"What can I do?" I asked Detective Warren.

Bettina was handling the gardening and hedge-trimming while I ran the investigation from the dining room table, which now had the box of flyers, clear plastic folders, push pins, tape and newspaper clippings about the disappearance.

"You could distribute flyers in the Taconic Road area and ask the homeowners to check their outbuildings," he replied.

I discovered a hidden world of homes accessible only through rambling private roads. One day I traipsed up a long drive, the lawn dotted with statues. The lake behind the house glinted in the sun, and through a picture window a large abstract painting peered down at me.

I left two flyers on the doorstep and turned back.

This had to be Meryl Streep's place. I knew the star had a lake-front home in Salisbury and that her husband was a sculptor.

The Taconic Road resident used to plough the snow from Daddy's road, but hadn't seen him in many years and was too far away to recognize the old man.

"He walked with difficulty, leading with the left leg, followed by the right, kind of dragging it, but not shuffling," he later told me. "His steps might have been a foot long. He was grey-haired and neither fat nor thin."

He knew it was between 7 and 8:30pm: there was nothing on TV, so he switched to the music channel, then to a TV show at 8:30. He had never seen the old man before or since.

I hiked from Daddy's house to the Taconic Road sighting, first via the conservation road—by then, mowed—and then via Daddy's drive. In the heat both routes took me well over an hour and wiped me out. I didn't believe Daddy could have made this journey on foot; but if he had, it would have taken him at least four times as long as me, thereby contradicting Pamela's account. But perhaps Pamela had taken him on an outing, they had argued and he got out of the car—after all, her nearest relative lived right off Taconic Road, which was also the quickest route to her family in Falls Village.

Or perhaps it was simply another old man. Searchers on foot and horseback combed the area with canines, but the dogs never picked up Daddy's scent. Two weekends later the police would stop Saturday evening traffic at the intersections of Route 41 and Hammertown, and Taconic and Twin Lakes Roads to see if a regular driver had spotted an elderly man on foot—no sightings.

• • •

Two weeks missing

I took a break from posting flyers. Mid-morning I stood at the open kitchen door. Matt had gone grocery shopping. Bettina was on the patio, reading. Dandy, a one-person cat, had warmed to Bettina and sat nearby, scrutinizing a hummingbird gliding towards the sugar water feeder. In the distance deer grazed on the lawn. A buzzing: a small low-flying plane emerged from nowhere. It circled lower and hovered above us. I realized it was looking for a body, filming. I flung myself out the door, down the patio steps, running in a circle beneath it, shrieking, cursing, punching at the plane with my fist. Bettina and Dandy sat silently watching.

Later, Bettina and I wrapped ourselves in towels and strolled to the stream. We scooped our hands and drank the water, my ritual whenever I visited. Then, feet sliding and slipping over the smooth-stoned bottom, we groped our way to a small swimming hole, three to four feet deep and five feet across. The water was icy cold, but once I made the plunge it was so invigorating that my worries evaporated. We swam back and forth alongside shoals of tiny fish. Then, lying on my back, arms stretched out across a fallen branch, I listened to the babbling water and gazed up through the pattern of green leaves to the wispy clouds, so gauzy I could almost see through them to the blue beyond.

The police finally interviewed Pamela's husband Steve, to my relief. The police told Steve that Dianna—Steve and Pamela's adult daughter, almost nineteen when Daddy vanished—said Pamela had called her the afternoon of Daddy's disappearance and told her Daddy was missing and she needed help. Dianna—witness one—claimed she had asked Steve—witness two—to help search for Daddy. Steve confirmed this. He recalled "that late in the day, he thought in the late afternoon," Pamela phoned and spoke with Dianna, who then "told him that Drew was missing and asked if he would help in the search." But Steve had to pick up his other children and couldn't help. Couldn't the police have confirmed what time Steve picked up his kids to help build a time frame?

What if Dianna, concerned, had called other people to help with the search? What if she herself had helped? Dianna had told troopers about the afternoon call, but there was no indication in the police records that detectives interviewed her. Couldn't they have interviewed her and checked the cell and landline records of the people who'd received the 1:17 and 1:22 calls from Daddy's house to see if outgoing distress calls had then been made to Pamela's family or friends?

After speaking with Steve, Detective Warren re-interviewed Pamela that same afternoon. Although Steve and Dianna had both referred to an *afternoon* distress call and Daddy's phone records supported that possibility, the detective accepted Pamela's claim that she had called people about the disappearance after the police were notified—not before. Daddy's phone records also showed calls to her family made after the 8:14 pm call to the police.

A year later, I would read the detective's report:

"Telephone records ... indicate that the telephone call to [Dianna] occurred ... at 2041 hours, after Troop B had been notified of Drew's disappearance."

He didn't mention the afternoon calls.

• • •

Three weeks missing

Pamela was again re-interviewed, this time by Detective Sorrento with another colleague. They asked her to verbally recount the events of the day Daddy disappeared, but, at her request, let her write her account. She now recalled reading Daddy several news articles in the morning, said he had watched TV in the afternoon while she did paperwork in the kitchen and they'd then walked briefly in the front yard. She also acknowledged, for the first time, that Daddy hadn't wanted her around. Sometimes, she wrote, "he'd say he didn't need me, that it was his house and that it was 'time for me [Pamela] to leave.'"

That day, as well, he had wanted her to leave. Two years after the disappearance I finally saw a photo of her: unkempt hair, shapeless T-shirt, stolid body, rigid face—no Marilyn Monroe. Daddy admired well-groomed people who valued their appearance, and I knew instantly he would have disliked her.

"We had spent a little time in the front yard, it was about 5:30 pm because he'd said it was 'time for you [Pamela] to go home' ... About 7:15 pm, Tom went to the bathroom I thought downstairs but was back in a minute with his *beige light coat* on." At the end of her statement, she added that he was wearing a *"light weight beige jacket."* So the tan or maybe brown or white jacket had become a *beige coat* and then a *beige jacket*.

Aware that Daddy hadn't liked Pamela, I wondered whether they'd argued and something had happened. Is that why she was now acknowledging he hadn't wanted her there? Her admission might have prompted the police to question her about their relationship. But no. The detective's summary suggested he hadn't picked up on any of these small but, in my view, revealing changes. However, he raised the possibility of a polygraph.

The next week Detective Sorrento asked her to take a polygraph. She agreed, emailing the lawyer handling her intermittent divorce proceedings and her town clerk sister saying she would be "taking a five question YN polygraph test … This is supposed to alleviate family concerns, improve my integrity, oh joy."

But the following day she called Detective Sorrento and said she had changed her mind. She didn't want to end up like Peter Reilly.

"Who's Peter Reilly?" I said, when Detective Warren, sounding flustered, called with the news.

"It's an old case. Controversial."

• • •

Joan Barthel's *A Death in Canaan* and Donald Connery's *Guilty until Proven Innocent* analyzed the case.

In 1973 eighteen-year-old Reilly was accused of the murder of his mother Barbara Gibbons, who lived in Falls Village. Troop B handled the case.

Born in Germany and schooled in England and New York City, Gibbons moved to Falls Village in 1955 after the birth of her son. Single, intelligent, well-educated and well-read, Gibbons was the quintessential outsider, breaching the norms of proper female behavior. A heavy drinker, bisexual, she once even had a live-in black boyfriend, to the consternation of the locals.

Her son came home one evening to find her bloody and sexually mutilated body. The house was awash in evidence—none of it pointing to Reilly. That didn't matter in the face of police preconceptions. They prejudged Reilly because he didn't cry that night—he showed his shock by shaking, not crying. Many troopers were contemptuous of Gibbons.

"Good riddance to bad rubbish," they said derisively. Wouldn't Reilly have wanted to get rid of his eccentric mom, they speculated. Highly impressionable, eager to please, Reilly took a polygraph test, presuming it would prove his innocence. Barthel quotes the taped interview:

"Do you have a clear recollection of what happened last night?" a trooper asks Reilly

"Yes."

"Is there any doubt in your mind, Pete?"

"I didn't understand that last question."

"I was just trying to probe your subconscious."

Later, smoking cigarettes together, the trooper again asks,

"Is there any doubt in your mind, right now, that you hurt your mother last night?"

"The test is giving me doubt right now. Disregarding the test, I still don't think I hurt my mother."

"But you have a doubt, don't you?"

"Yes. I've been drilled and drilled and drilled ... I'm losing all memory now because I'm getting tired. But he [another trooper] did tell me that I could have forgotten. That really shook me."

For eight hours four troopers took turns grilling Reilly. Connery describes the scene, in which one trooper told the boy: "we'll take you and we'll lock you up and treat you like an animal." Insisting he had killed her, the troopers proposed *possible murder scenarios*. Exhausted, dazed, denied sleep and food, the boy confessed.

"I definitely did do what happened to my mother last night. But the thing that I don't realize is the exact steps that I took doing it," Connery quotes him.

Based purely on the confession, and without any physical evidence, Reilly was convicted of manslaughter and began serving his sentence.

Brave journalists exposed the injustice towards the boy who'd been prejudged; playwright Arthur Miller gave his support. New evidence came to light. The police had withheld evidence; the prosecutor had failed to share evidence with the defense. Reilly's confession had been psychologically coerced; he had accepted the police version of a *possible scenario*. He was exonerated. Even then, despite overwhelming evidence to the contrary, the state police continued to insist that their original misconception was correct.

His mother's murder remains unsolved.

Just eight years before the Reilly affair, Troop B had a false confession case in the small Litchfield County town of Barkhamsted. This concerned young homemaker and mother Dorothy Thompson, found viciously beaten and hanging in her home, later dying in hospital. Two rival detectives obtained confessions, one from the victim's mentally disturbed mother-in-law, the other from nineteen-year-old handyman Harry Solberg. The case was dissected in Mildred Savage's prize-winning tome, *A Great Fall*.

"I killed her. That's what you want," Solberg confessed after a lengthy interrogation in which the police put forward a *possible scenario*. "I just can't remember what actually took place. I don't actually remember what happened."

The similarities in Reilly's and Solberg's statements were astonishing—each confessing to a killing, neither remembering the details.

Solberg was twice brought to trial, with the first detective testifying for his defense. He was convicted of writing a false confession, but not of Thompson's murder, which is also unsolved.

I desperately wanted to fill in the gaps about the day Daddy was reported missing. But given Troop B's history of extracting false confessions, perhaps Pamela had reason for concern. Still, I reflected, wasn't it a stretch to compare herself to Peter Reilly?

Jack called. I told him Pamela had refused to take a polygraph.

"You'd think she'd want to help if she has nothing to hide," he replied.

CHAPTER 7

Pamela sent a card to the house addressed to me, Bettina and Matt. It depicted a wooded scene and came in a matching envelope, postmarked August 3, the day she and her husband were each interviewed. She had written:

"We all wish I had followed him the moment he said he was going out. I'm sure everyone is more aware now of what a few minutes can make or of keeping a closer eye on ones with special care needs. I hope we can each find peace knowing what a bright soul Tom is."

Was this Pamela's idea of an apology? Her stress on the collective rather than her own responsibility and her presentation of the disappearance as a learning experience were disturbing and distressing. So was her apparent assumption that Daddy was in the woods and that people would believe her pat account—particularly after she had refused to take a polygraph. I found it manipulative. It reinforced my antipathy towards her, and I knew that if I met her—I hadn't—I would turn and flee.

She was worried we might sue her, it transpired. She spoke to an attorney friend who advised her that "the best defense is a strong offense," she emailed her family later that month. We were probably trying to use her as a scapegoat, she added.

• • •

Crisscrossing the Tri-State area, I put up 500 flyers that summer. Leaving the house around 9 am, I would return, dehydrated and exhausted, around 5pm.

One day I put up flyers in Salisbury village. Kay, who owned a local restaurant, approached me.

"Your father used to eat in my restaurant. When he was justice of the peace he married me and my husband. But he got so demented he never recognized me."

Caught off guard, I stood stunned, silent. *My father's not demented*, I wanted to say. *He has dementia.* Daddy and I used to go to her restaurant whenever I visited. The last time, just six months before he vanished, he was ninety.

Each time, as we waited to be served, he would lean across the table and murmur:

"I know her. I think her name's Kay. I married her and her husband. I heard they're not together anymore. I don't think she remembers me."

We always tried to catch Kay's eye, but she sailed by, stony-faced. Daddy was undoubtedly the best-dressed man in Salisbury and always wore a suit or smart sweater when we ate there. It was a popular establishment, and I used to think her coldness was the pressure of work. Now I know better. Dementia, it seemed, was her convenient rationale for having snubbed him.

Another day I found myself in tiny Falls Village, Connecticut's second-smallest town and a historic district with a forgotten history of violence dating long before the Gibbons murder. James Mars was born a slave there, owned by a congregational minister. Much later people told Mars "they did not know that slavery was ever allowed in Connecticut, and some affirm that it never did exist in the State." So in 1868 he published his *Life of James Mars, a Slave Born and Sold in Connecticut* to rectify this historical amnesia.

Falls Village's official name is Canaan—but it's nicknamed after the town's principal village to avoid being muddled with North Canaan or East Canaan—the locals like the confusion this causes outsiders. Like North Canaan, it had once prospered, with its own thriving general store. But those days were long gone.

I parked the car at the bottom of Main Street. The heat felt heavy. Looking up the street, on my right was the old Falls Village Inn, and on my left, the Town Hall, with a sign proclaiming Town of Canaan, Falls Village. Small buildings dotted the street, which was otherwise empty, eerily silent, frozen in time. Despite the quaint façades, a sense of inbreeding and decay smacked me in the face.

We do not give up our secrets easily, the village seemed to be whispering.

Plucking up courage, I left a flyer in the Town Hall—was that Pamela's sister with the queasy smile?

Back outside, I tacked up a second flyer on a poster board.

A drunk stumbled out of the nearby liquor store, the shopkeeper on his heels.

"Oh, I heard about him," the drunk said, frowning at the flyer. "He escaped from his fenced-in yard and *wandered* off."

Escaped and wandered off? So that's what they're saying in Falls Village.

"You must have the wrong man. There's no fence in his yard, and he wasn't a prisoner. People were employed to go with him if he wanted to go out. Anyway, he was too weak to go far." I heard myself challenging the fictional Falls Village claim, hoping that at least the shopkeeper would listen.

Privately, several Connecticut Canine Search and Rescue handlers questioned whether Daddy had really left on foot. One of them told me they were checking possible dump sites. Pamela could have taken him with her and left him alone, as she had when he had waved to Jonathan outside St Mary's Church. Perhaps, bored, he left the car. Maybe someone picked him up.

Just in case, I posted queries on an online motorcycle site and took the train to Grand Central Station in New York City, dashing out at each stop to hastily stick up a flyer. In Grand Central, I looked into the blue eyes of an old toothless homeless man, probably someone's father. Daddy had blue eyes and wore dentures.

Are you my father?

I was too shy to ask. I wish I had; his face still haunts me.

Late August I flew to Georgia to visit Daddy's family. I hadn't seen them for decades. As children Bettina and I spent every summer in Georgia. But then my parents began taking us to Cape Cod and Nantucket. A teenager, I didn't grasp what a loss this was. But I realized it when I arrived: I'm a Yankee, yet tied to the South. I visited Aunt

Mildred, still slim and trim. Her memory was crystal clear, but she lived with nineteen dogs, it transpired—the cats slept outside. So we chatted out front—it was hot as an oven. I saw all the cousins, and late one afternoon we discussed Daddy's case over hamburgers and Coke. Most of them believed the two employees were lying, but Mildred, in a smart sleeveless summer sheath, obstinately defended Matt, who still called her.

• • •

Back in Salisbury I resumed putting up flyers. I met with Detective Warren at his office to show him Pamela's card. After reading the card, he wanted to keep the original and so made me a copy. We briefly discussed the case. He mentioned they'd checked ATM videotapes in case Daddy had tried to withdraw money. But Daddy had never used an ATM machine in his life.

Pamela's name came up.

"I've had dealings with her before," he said, "but this is the first time it's been something of this order."

"I don't understand." I felt my heart sink. "Are you saying you've had dealings with her before in your capacity as an officer of the law?"

"Yes, but never anything of this order." He spoke slowly, carefully. "Each time she has placed the blame for whatever's happened on someone else."

An officer of the law. Replaying that scene in my mind, I realize I had genuinely believed then that the police strove to uphold the law. Indeed, I took it for granted. Of course, the police were a non-presence in my white upper-middle-class Larchmont childhood, when my knowledge of them came from TV. First was the thrilling legal drama *Perry Mason*, in which the suave Los Angeles defense attorney invariably got his client off, demonstrating that police and prosecutors could make mistakes and that the wrongly accused could attain justice—if they were white, of course; only once did I see Perry Mason defend a non-white client. Another favorite was the eponymously-named *Andy Griffith Show* in which the actor played widowed sheriff Andy Taylor of fictional small town Mayberry, North Carolina. An All-American honest cop who solved problems with reason, Sheriff Taylor kept peace amongst the locals through home-spun advice and mediation, while cracking down on moonshiners and keeping out-of-town criminals at bay, the occasional black characters silent and in the background.

A far cry from the world of Ava DuVernay, director of the Oscar-nominated documentary *13th* about America's racially-biased criminal justice system. DuVernay grew up in Compton, California, where she experienced a "heavy police presence," she told Oprah Winfrey.

She recalled, as a child, "not feeling safety when I would see police, feeling fear, feeling they were coming after me, or coming after the people in my neighborhood."

"Growing up, the police represented danger, fear?" Oprah asked.

"Yes," DuVernay replied, whereas "many people think safety, they think relief, they think 'the good guy.'"

• • •

My first encounter with the *real* police came in the early 1970s. Nineteen, living in Johnson City, New York, I had woken up to hear several boys speaking in muffled tones outside my door. Opening the door, I caught the neighbor's young boys and their friend pouring kerosene over my kitten. One had a box of matches in his hand.

"What are you doing!?"

I grabbed the kitten, shampooed it and called the vet.

I felt I should find an authority figure to speak to them. I couldn't reach their mother—a single working mom, and the local minister wouldn't help. I called the police and explained the situation. Two police officers arrived and told the boys in a firm but fatherly tone that this must never happen again. Of course, their mother stopped speaking to me. But the cops were genuinely trying to be helpful. Perhaps in those days there was still some sense of community policing—in white areas, at least.

My second encounter was in Los Angeles in the 1980s, when I had seen a prowler outside my ground-floor window. I called the cops, and sometime later two Los Angeles Police Department officers knocked on my door. When I opened it, they stood at opposite angles across from me, their hands on their guns. They were polite, but their nervousness was contagious, and I was relieved to see them leave. The third occasion concerned my visa application for apartheid South Africa. For this I needed official confirmation I did not have a criminal record. This required a trip to the Los Angeles Police Department, where an officer ran a computer check on me.

"This carries a lot of clout," said the secretary when she handed me the official letter confirming my unblemished record. Indeed, it did the trick.

• • •

Like most middle-class white Americans, I believed in my country's institutions, while nonetheless recognizing they were flawed. I believed that the detective sitting in front of me *wanted* to find Daddy and close the case, and I ascribed the investigative shortcomings to inexperience.

Shortly before I left for England, the detective finally conceded that Pamela's account of the time was highly questionable.

"The probability is in the very high nineties—we can't be 100 per cent certain without a body—that Tom didn't leave the house in the evening. If we'd known he'd left earlier, we would have done a different type of search. We're now working on the assumption he could have left any time after 1 pm."

"Why 1 pm?"

"In the event Matt was confused about the time he left the house. I'm sure now, with the hunting season approaching and the foliage thinning out, his remains will be found."

"Isn't it conceivable my father could have been driven off his property?"

"Yes," he replied sheepishly.

He couldn't meet my eyes.

September, preparing to head back to England, I strolled to the stream and stared at the gushing water splashing over the stones. I scooped my hands and drank, then headed back towards the house. But reaching the lawn, I collapsed. A shriek surged from my gut, erupting out of my mouth.

"*Ahhhhh … I'm sorry Daddy, I'm sorry Daddy.*"

I lay silently. Another shriek.

"*Ahhhhh … I'm sorry Daddy, forgive me, Daddy, forgive me.*"

I continued shrieking until I was empty.

I lay still for some time, then rose and plodded to the house, passing Dandy, eyeing me from the front steps.

That afternoon I forced myself to make two phone calls.

The first was to Matt's girlfriend, Anna.

"Oh Allison. I didn't know if I should call or not. Tom was so charming. He always flattered me. But he's in a better place now."

Better place? What place? How could you say he's in a better place when we don't know where he is? He could be homeless somewhere!

Again and again that summer, I had heard people making pronouncements about what had happened—when they knew even less than I did. I would listen as they advised me what to believe. My thoughts, my feelings were still bottled inside me. I couldn't express them.

Instead, pen in hand, I focused on my prepared questions:

"Can you tell me what you remember of that day?"

"When I got off the train, I was surprised Tom wasn't with Matt because he normally brings him along when he meets me. I asked, 'Where's Tom?' He said he left him with Pamela. We got back to the house around 7:30, 7:40. It was still bright outside. Pamela was walking quickly into the garage. She was holding something in her hand. It looked like a flashlight.

"Matt asked, 'Where's Tom?'

"She said, 'I thought he was upstairs. He must have stepped out. I'm looking for him.'

"Matt blurted: 'How can you be so stupid as to let someone in his condition go out without following him?'

"She got upset: 'I'm just going out. He must be out there. It was just ten minutes.'

"I told Matt to calm down. He was upsetting Pamela. 'Let's look for him,' I said. After all, how far could he have gotten in ten minutes?"

Hurriedly taking notes, I paused to ponder why Anna should worry that Matt was upsetting Pamela. Didn't she understand Matt was in a panic because he was close to Daddy, responsible for him?

Anna said Matt and Pamela went to the footbridge over the stream, then she and Matt drove to the top of Ravine Ridge Road and up Route 41.

To my amazement, she began praising Pamela:

"She's so demure. She's a mother."

I couldn't fathom how she could defend the woman responsible for Daddy's disappearance.

Dismayed, I hung up.

I silently gathered my thoughts. Then I picked up my pen and called Karen Kisslinger, the woman who'd given Pamela a reference.

"Are you aware my father disappeared, Karen?"

"Yes, Pamela told me. She said it could have happened to anyone." Karen paused, choosing her words with care. "I knew she had personal problems, but I thought because it was just filling in that she would be okay. She cared for my children when they were small."

"How long ago was that?" She inhaled.

"Eighteen years."

"Did you tell Matt that?"

She took another breath.

"No ... Matt never had a problem with her," she said, her voice rising defensively. "Is he *still* missing?"

"Yes. He's still missing."

CHAPTER 8

The United States was gearing up for its 2008 presidential primaries. Back in York, I began working with Bettina's friend Peter to contact soup kitchens and shelters in the Tri-State area. I emailed or faxed, and Peter, who lived in New York City, followed up with phone calls. I didn't expect to find anything, but it was still important to rule out the possibility that Daddy had been lost elsewhere and picked up. Like Sherlock Holmes' curious incident of the dog that didn't bark, it was increasingly clear to me that Daddy had left no traces of walking from his home to a vehicle road precisely because he hadn't. The absence of evidence was itself evidence.

My academic work continued—a conference in Washington, DC in early January, a research trip to South Africa during the spring break, another conference in Quebec City in May.

I was fascinated by Algeria, a former French settler society with striking similarities to South Africa. Both countries had been subject to military conquest and massive land expropriation. They both had rigid social divisions—South Africa along color lines, and Algeria, religious lines. They also shared socialist and communist traditions. Having finished my Bunting biography, I began working on a book about the Algerian communist party.

Like Daddy, I was a volunteer. I had been listening to York primary school children read, assessing their reading and comprehension. I truly enjoyed the work and wanted to gain experience with children in the hopes of adoption. Once the adoption agency learned Daddy was missing, however, they dropped me like a hot potato.

The social worker came to my house and without preliminaries announced that the agency wanted me to withdraw my application. I refused; later that week they wrote stating they had dropped me. Not only did I face stigma as a single woman seeking to adopt, I was now tainted by my connection to a missing person. If they thought I would be too preoccupied with the disappearance to care for an adopted child, why didn't they say so? Or did they think the disappearance was my fault? I didn't have the stamina to contest it.

• • •

Four months missing

Detective Warren had suggested Bettina and I depose Pamela to get more details from her about the day Daddy disappeared. To do this, we would have to take out a civil suit against her for negligence. A deposition is pretrial out-of-court oral testimony transcribed for use in court. It preserves witness recollections and provides a baseline from which later court testimony can be checked for inconsistencies. Discovery allows the parties in a legal dispute to collect and preview evidence from each other, by, for example, providing answers in depositions and producing documents.

We approached a law firm in Litchfield, the former county seat until Connecticut abolished county governments in 1960. Litchfield was home to the country's first law school, founded in 1784, and to one of its earliest women's educational institutions, established in 1792. The town that grew up around the village green flourished in the late eighteenth century, reflecting its highly educated population—the abolitionist Harriet Beecher Stowe, for one, author of *Uncle Tom's Cabin*, grew up there. But lacking sufficient water supply and rail links for industry, its fortunes had declined over the nineteenth century. Nonetheless, its elegant colonial homes with their distinctive black shutters suggested a community in which wealth passed easily from one generation to the next.

Our lawyer, poised and polished, filed a negligence complaint on behalf of Daddy, the plaintiff. This argued that the defendant, Pamela, "was negligent in carrying out her duties to the plaintiff in that she failed to exercise the reasonable care of one who undertakes to care for an elderly man with dementia and poor balance, such as the plaintiff."

The complaint explained that:

"a. She allowed the plaintiff to leave his home unattended and unsupervised; b. She failed to accompany the plaintiff when he left the home; c. She focused more on the television program she was watching than on her duty to care for and supervise the plaintiff; d. She failed to remain aware of the plaintiff's actions and his whereabouts; e. She failed to recognize that the plaintiff was not in the home within a reasonable time of his departure from the home; f. She failed to report to the police that the plaintiff was missing within a reasonable time from when she became aware that the plaintiff was not in the home; g. She failed to report to the police that the plaintiff was missing within a reasonable time of his departure from the home."

Daddy had been damaged in numerous ways as a result of her negligence, the complaint contended:

"a. He has endured being lost and displaced from his home and familiar people and surroundings; b. He has suffered emotional distress, fear, humiliation, panic and confusion at being unable to find his way back home; c. He has been prevented from enjoying the pleasure and comfort of communicating, sharing and socializing with his daughters and friends; d. He has lost the comfort and enjoyment of his home, where he had wished to live for the remainder of his life; e. He has suffered bodily harm from being exposed to the natural elements, weather, and the lack of shelter, nourishment and his medications."

Pamela was summoned to our lawyer's office and asked to bring along emails, other writings and anything else that comprised evidence.

Scheduling the deposition proved difficult. Having refused to take a polygraph, Pamela didn't want to answer any more questions about Daddy's disappearance. Unknown to us, her personal life was falling apart. On the very day Daddy's negligence complaint was filed, her husband Steve filed for divorce. Despite Steve's statement to the police that he believed his wife's account of Daddy's vanishing, he clearly had misgivings about her behavior. Even before the disappearance, he had started, then dropped, divorce proceedings.

But since Daddy's disappearance her behavior seemed to have become increasingly bizarre. A week after the disappearance she emailed her friends claiming her husband had started arguing about divorce, they'd had a blazing row and his mother had asked her to see a psychiatrist.

She mentioned Daddy at the end, a seeming afterthought, adding, "only headaches from his daughters sadly." Although we had never tried to contact her—I wanted nothing to do with her—it seemed she was still trying to present herself as the misunderstood victim.

Three months after the disappearance Steve filed for custody of their three minor children and for exclusive use of the marital home acquired through his employment, claiming that Pamela was "extremely disruptive, volatile, and poses a potential danger to the Plaintiff and the minor children." Then came the divorce suit. Steve asked that the court appoint a *guardian ad litem* to assist in determining appropriate custody of and access to the children. Less than two weeks later Steve and Pamela agreed to joint legal custody with the stipulation that neither party would discuss the divorce in front of the children or make disparaging comments about the other.

Pamela was juggling Daddy's complaint and her husband's divorce suit. She agreed to vacate the family home in January; curiously, I would later learn, she went walking right next to Daddy's property that same day. Two weeks later she called our lawyer proposing mediation. That wasn't the point: we needed to know what had happened the day Daddy vanished. Our lawyer sent a notice of deposition. The court granted her husband's request and ordered that a *guardian ad litem* be appointed for her children and that Family Services do a custody evaluation. Pamela left our lawyer long muddled messages. The deposition was rescheduled. Our lawyer served her with a subpoena. In March 2008, almost eight months after the disappearance, Pamela was finally deposed at our lawyer's office.

• • •

"You arrived at what time on the morning of 21st July?" our lawyer began.

"9:30."

"And then when did Matt leave the premises?"

"7:15 p.m. ... I am on Tom. Matt left ... if I can refer to my notes because ... Okay. Let's see it—doesn't say when he left exactly, but I think it was—usually he would leave around 11:00."

"Do you recall having lunch with Mr. Drew that day?"

"With Mr. Drew, yes."

"Had Matt already left by lunch time?"

"I think—yes. I think so, but—this is eight or nine months ago."

"Had your personal life been interfering with your ability to care for Mr. Drew?" the lawyer enquired.

"Not in terms of, you know, watching shows with him and making meals. I would journal sometimes or talk to my mother-in-law sometimes on the phone. I check in on my kids."

She told our attorney she kept an online journal, so perhaps she had a laptop with her, unless she used Matt's computer.

The lawyer moved on to Daddy's condition.

"How fast could he move?"

"In the—when we started, he could move pretty well, but we would walk, maybe—there is a bridge on the driveway, or a bridge out to the side … Maybe we would walk together that far, but after he fell … he could not walk that far at all outside."

"Could you describe how he appeared when walking?"

"Slow. And I felt more comfortable giving him a hand of support, because I just felt, outdoors, he had been kneeling down earlier in the day"—she had not previously mentioned that—"and the knees, you know—I tend to hover. I help people, who I don't know, get up sometimes … So that is just kind of my style. But he didn't mind."

Crucially, she couldn't—or wouldn't—account for the day except at some point, she claimed, Daddy trimmed the back patio hedges, ate lunch and spent about ten minutes in the front yard before eating dinner.

"Then the two of you were alone all afternoon?"

"Yes … We basically spent more time than usual out on the patio." Later, I would read that her first email after the disappearance stated "an hour or more." In summer Daddy generally spent most of the day outside—as he had when Bettina visited in June.

"I read him a poem. He said—he made me laugh. He said I should—and I said 'publish?' He said, 'publish it.' That was sweet. Another man told me something similar, who also since died."

I noted her use of *also*—she believed or possibly knew Daddy was dead—and her acknowledgement to having been alone with Daddy all afternoon, again raised a question about Matt's claim to have left at 3 pm.

And then?

"I think we went inside—I am trying to think if there was a movie on … We would always watch Lifetime or AMC or whatever, so we probably went inside and watched something in the afternoon"—she was speaking *hypothetically* rather than about what had actually happened.

"I am asking not what you might have done but if, sitting here today, you can recall on that day what the two of you did?"

"I can't a hundred percent say, but we sometimes sat at the kitchen table and visited." Another *hypothetical* response.

"Okay. Then sometime—well, after coming inside, you don't recall exactly what you did, but ultimately you did prepare dinner."

"Right."

"Do you know when you started to prepare dinner?"

"Yes."

"Okay. I am asking you not to look at your notes, but the best you can, with your own independent recollection now, what you remember."

"After four days of—two days of real stress that is almost like this all over again, I just feel it's really unfair to ask that question. I just do."

The lawyer referred to Mildred's call:

"It's my understanding that Mr. Drew's sister, Mildred, called on the day he disappeared," the lawyer stated. "Do you recall her calling?"

"Quite possible. I think so, now that you are saying it. I couldn't tell you off the top of my head, but she called sometimes, and quite possibly that day."

"But you don't remember her calling?"

"I am thinking maybe in the afternoon, sitting on the couch, you know, easily accessible to the phone."

"Actually Mr. Drew wasn't permitted to speak with his sister. Is any of this jogging your memory?" the lawyer asked.

"Mr. Drew wasn't permitted?"

"My understanding is she called about noon time."

"Uh-huh."

"Asked to speak with Mr. Drew but was refused."

"Uh-huh. Maybe he was—I don't. I mean, she has called before. Maybe I am remembering another time. I know he has spoken to her, and that is usually the setup." She hastened to explain:

"I am thinking possibly if he was out on the porch, because I think we did stay a little longer outdoors, like past noon for lunch time, you know. So for him to get from the patio inside would have been a bit much, would have taken like, I don't know, five minutes or something. She is from Georgia, and I wouldn't want to rush him, not the kind of thing I am going to run to the phone."

"It would have been reasonable for—in your memory it would have been reasonable for you to maybe have suggested a call back at a different time?"

"Yes … I wouldn't say you can't talk to him, you know, like that, but maybe he was out on the patio, so, yes." Once again, she was speaking *hypothetically*, as if she didn't actually know what had happened. Was she really the woman Aunt Mildred spoke to that Saturday?

In the afternoon she and Daddy went out to the front yard for ten minutes.

"And then he was saying, 'When are you going to go home? Isn't it time for you to go home now?' I said, 'In a little while. In an hour or so when Matt is back.'"

She repeated that point, stressing that when they were out in front Daddy kept asking when she was going to leave.

"That's when Tom asked me when I am going home. And I realized it was about 5:30, and I said in about an hour, after dinner, when Matt comes home. So, I felt good that I remembered it was 5:30 at that point, because when we went in we ate dinner a little bit later, for some reason, probably 6:00, 6:15 or 6:30."

Why did she think it was 5:30? Was she wearing a watch?

"I was just estimating." And she reiterated:

"He would get anxious if he thought I was moving in. It was his home, and—I think I need a bathroom break."

They resumed the questioning after a short break. She wasn't sure what happened next.

"We might have watched another little bit of a show, and then we had dinner around, I think 6:15."

"Sitting here today, are you unsure of the time?"

"No. I think I made it around 6:15 or 6:30 is when we were cleaning up. So it was just a little later than I thought it would be, for some reason. We started eating at 6:15 or 6:30."

After dinner they watched TV in the library.

"He was sitting next to me. He got up twice. At first I thought he was going to the bathroom, but he came back in with his coat on. So I realized he had his coat on, once he stood up and said, 'I have got to get going' … when I went to check, after about five minutes, the [front] door was locked, so I thought he went upstairs to the bathroom."

The alleged *jacket*, which she had variously described as tan, brown, white or beige, was once again a *coat*. But she could not recall what the coat looked like.

"I mean I didn't really notice that he had the coat on. Again, my mind isn't about what you are wearing. I thought maybe he just put it on because he is cold, kind of like I am doing now, just one of those extra layers. It was evening, so I mean, it wasn't out of the question to put on another layer."

Except no jacket or coat was missing.

Trooper Grant's initial report had stated that Pamela claimed to have seen Daddy leave through the kitchen doors. But now she said,

"Matt had said not to let him go out the sliding doors. I forget. The door didn't close well and/or, again, the balance. There is no railing there. It was always kind of a game to keep it locked, not let it be open if he is in the room in the early days."

To the contrary—Daddy normally went out through the kitchen doors, especially if he were gardening or sitting on the back patio, or through the garage, if he needed a tool or was going for a drive. In the summer's humidity the front door swelled and was harder to open. Why would she make such claims about the kitchen doors?

Notwithstanding her vagueness about the alleged jacket, she recalled his shoes.

"I seem to remember at the time that he had slip-ons, because sometimes he would—another time when he had those slip-ons on, he would almost get out of them. I even thought that night what if, you know—they were loose fitting. What if he got stuck and it slipped off and he went to reach for it and fell. You know, that is what I thought about, the shoes, more than I usually do."

Later, she returned to the shoes.

"I started to think about his shoes, if they got stuck in the muck or came off and he fell. There's a lot of reasons why he could fall."

Were the shoes a sign of something else, like the sliding kitchen doors? If Pamela or a friend moved the body, did she have to reach down and pick up his shoes? Her concern with Daddy's shoes and his possibly falling contradicted what I perceived as her cavalier attitude about his safety.

He'd fallen several times since she had been working for him, most recently in April, three months before the disappearance: leaning over in a kitchen chair to reach something on the counter, he had lost his balance and tumbled on the floor. Pamela knew about those falls and had acknowledged seeing his bruises. Matt had reminded the part-time companions to keep their eyes on Daddy when he moved. She herself had just claimed she "felt more comfortable giving him a hand."

"So it's your understanding that you were to monitor him more closely?" the lawyer asked.

"A little more closely."

"Had you, yourself, noticed issues with Mr. Drew's balance?"

"Not too much. You know, he may have held on to the counter or a chair a minute here or there, but not like stumbling or tripping."

And what did Pamela think had happened, the lawyer asked?

"What if somehow he got to the top of the road, someone might have hit him, because I heard people go fast on that road," she speculated. "I thought somebody is trying to cover it up. I know it was searched pretty close … there would be some blood on some clothing or something, but you know, you just don't know … I feel like there is probably an element of foul play, if he made it to the road, then. And like, what if he reached out for help for the light? Like help, and step in front of a car or something, whatever. I thought if anybody knows and they are not telling, it's probably because there is wrongdoing on that end."

Now she became vague, professing to have forgotten other details about the day. When asked about the inconsistencies in her statements in the police reports, she protested:

"Somebody transcribed it wrong."

"At any time after July 21, have you been upstairs in the Drew house?

"No."

"Did you delete any messages from the caller ID since Mr. Drew's disappearance?"

"No."

Yet she was now willing to have her car trunk inspected; in fact, she suggested it.

"Would you be willing to let the police do that?"

"Sure."

They ended the session at lunchtime and set a date to reconvene.

CHAPTER 9

A week after Daddy was reported missing, Pamela recounted a dream about him in her online journal. She gave us a copy as part of the discovery process, so I only read it nine months after the disappearance. "He was home wanting to wash his feet and get into bed," she began.

"I was happy to go find the wash basin and four small towels. As I was getting one wet, I noticed something behind a dresser with high legs. It looked like an arm. I quickly checked and it seemed like a skeleton. Then I froze with fear. I'd found Tom. I ran to tell [Matt] ... but before I could tell him, he told me to patiently wait. I went back, shaking off the fear enough to kneel down and look closely. It seemed too far along to be Tom's ... As I finally got close enough to almost touch the skeleton, I realized it was a manekan [sic], made from stockings and scraps and wire. I suddenly laughed. Tom was a fashion designier [sic], and this must have been one of his old manekans [sic]! It looked so real, but at least it wasn't what I had thought. When [Matt] came to ask me what had turned me white as a ghost, I laughed, and said, 'Oh, it's nothing. I was mistaken.'"

Skeletons in dreams can be interpreted as symbolizing a guilty secret—the proverbial skeleton in the closet. Did Pamela feel culpable? Was she suppressing the events of the day—is that why she couldn't recollect them? Like her reference to "another man ... who also since died," she seemed certain at the time of the dream that Daddy was dead. The image of the washing of feet is laden with Christian symbolism, although Pamela wasn't claiming to have washed Daddy's feet, but to have provided him with the means to do so himself.

• • •

Pamela's second deposition took place three weeks after the first, the same day her husband Steve filed a motion for immediate sole custody of the children. Hoping I might glean more insight into what had happened on the day Daddy was reported missing, I drove to the Litchfield County Courthouse, right across from the village green, to look at the divorce proceedings. I passed under its imposing clock tower and through its arched entrance. Inside, a clerk pointed me to a room on the right, where I requested the file and set up my laptop on an empty table to take notes. She brought me the file, and I began reading.

"Over the past several weeks," Steve maintained, Pamela "has become increasingly erratic, bizarre, and unpredictable. It is the Plaintiff's belief that she is in need of intensive in-patient psychiatric care." He explained that she "has consistently and repeatedly gotten into physical confrontations with the minor children and accuses them of being abusive towards her ... consistently and repeatedly spoken about the divorce and adult matters directly with the children, including talking to the children about violence, murder, and suicide."

Reading these words, I felt nauseous. Of course, emotions run high in divorce cases. How could I know how accurate her husband's account was? Nonetheless, the words jarred me, and I couldn't help imagining something violent happening to Daddy, even if hiding the body in panic or fear of blame.

Pamela left the marital home, as agreed, and was shifting between house-sitting and staying with a relative in Falls Village. She would show up at Steve's house, "refusing to leave the premises when the Plaintiff and/or children request that she do so, baiting them by telling them to call the police if they want her to leave." She asserted that their youngest daughter had "mental problems" and asked her school "to put her in a special program for mentally disturbed children." Yet the school principal and guidance counselor described the girl as "a bright, well-behaved child who exhibits no signs of a mental disorder."

Pamela seemed determined to sabotage Steve's employment, he claimed, even though he was the sole breadwinner. Sometimes, she marched into his workplace, "disrupting the working atmosphere with threats of trying to get the Plaintiff and his boss fired based on trumped up accusations that have no merit." She was "volunteering for non-paying jobs or attending workshops and seminars," sometimes ignoring her parenting responsibilities to attend those sessions. She even said she "would move into a homeless shelter with the children rather than look for employment."

Her husband asked for sole legal and physical custody:

"The children have repeatedly told the Plaintiff that they do not want to reside or even see their mother because she acts 'crazy' and they are frightened of her."

• • •

Our lawyer began the second deposition by going over Pamela's discovery documents.

"Now showing you Exhibit 15 from your deposition. What is that?"

"That is the night he was lost."

"This is an email that you wrote?"

"Yes." Pamela became agitated, upset. Was she going to cry?

"I'm sorry; but I do need to go into this a bit. Would you like to take a moment?"

"Yes."

"Why don't we go off the record for a bit?"

They took a five minute break. Pamela composed herself.

"And this was written the day of Mr. Drew's disappearance?" the lawyer resumed.

"Late at night, yes."

"On the message it actually identifies the time of twenty-one forty-six, do you see that?"

"Yes."

"Do you know when you wrote this message?"

"Well, it says it's just after midnight, and I think that's the—so I don't know if I'm responding to somebody. I think that's the original one. I don't know my military time."

"All right ... this would actually be 9:46 p.m.?"

"Yeah."

"But is it your recollection you actually wrote this after midnight?"

"Right. See how it says, '*RE Sat noon*'? I'm trying to think if I was responding to somebody or something, yeah."

Pamela's emails indicated that she and her relatives commonly used a day and time period as a subject line. Curiously, though, there were no other emails with the *Sat noon* subject in the batches she gave the lawyer, and I speculated whether she had weeded them out.

"Do you recall sending that message out?"

"Yeah."

"Do you recall where you were when you sent it out?"

"At my house."

"And you had been at the Drew residence until about 11:30 p.m. on that day, correct?"

"Yeah, yeah."

Presumably her first written account of the disappearance and the first written use of the term *wander* to describe Daddy's absence, the email stated:

"The man I care for wandered off for about 10 minutes, and we couldn't find him after a half hour of searching from 7:30 to 8 pm, so called the police and canine rescue ... I let him go out for about 5 minutes, but thought he went to the bathroom upstairs because the front door was locked. I waited another five or so, then checked in his bathroom after not getting an answer. The kitchen sliding door was open and that's when I realized he went out that way, where we had spent an hour or more during the day trimming hedges around the patio."

She continued: "I circled the whole area for about an hour or more, calling out, using my whistle and then again going out with an officer deeper into the woods." Perhaps she did go out for a while. But when Daddy's friend Woody came to search on the Sunday morning, a trooper spoke to him:

"Do you know the woman looking after him?"

"No. I knew Matt, but I never met her. She was part-time."

"While we were looking last night she sat on the couch reading the newspaper. I never saw anything like it. She should have been helping, but she sat there reading." And before the cops came she had been praying.

Before ending her email, Pamela thanked her sister Amelia, "for doing Noreen in the morning … On my way home, a deer ran into my side of the car, damaging the rim above the tire. I looked for the deer but I think it must have leapt forward or turned back." Amelia replied: "Nelly gave me $$ to give you for the hours you worked this weekend"—Nelly employed Pamela and other local women to look after her elderly mother Noreen. Pamela wrote back later Sunday morning that Tom had "had a good day overall" and "at least he had a jacket on."

As the lawyer pressed on, it became clear Pamela would go walking or jogging instead of providing Daddy with companionship.

She emailed Amelia on May 26 that she was "going to 'work' … Come by if you want to visit & walk," suggesting that she hadn't been serious about watching Daddy, hadn't seen her employment there as work.

"I would sometimes go for like a five, maybe even a ten minute walk—five minutes up and five minutes back—once during the whole time," she told the lawyer.

"You mentioned that on occasion you would take a short jog?"

"Yeah."

"Where would you jog?"

"Just up the drive toward the—toward the main road."

"And when you went for jogs, how long would you leave Mr. Drew unsupervised?"

"I'd say five to ten minutes tops. Sometimes I run all the way up; and after a while I realized, you know what, I could do two—you know, I could just keep it shorter, because I felt like this is too far." She hastened to add she hadn't left the house the day he was reported missing.

"Did you ever invite people over to the Drew residence when you were there working?" the lawyer asked.

"I did, just to see if they'd like to come and volunteer and stay with him." She mentioned two women. Once when a woman named Dolly came over, "I said would you stay with him while I go for a jog, and she said okay. So they were both just sitting there."

"I was kind of on the hunt," Pamela continued.

"When you say you were on the 'hunt,' you were looking for assistance in caring for him?"

"Yes."

"Coverage, so to speak?"

"Uh-huh. Yes. I'm wondering if I can take a bathroom break?"

They took a 17-minute break.

So despite being paid to watch Daddy, she had left him on his own while she went jogging and with someone else on some occasions. Maybe she had left him alone or with another person the day he had been reported missing. I found no indication the police had checked with Dolly.

I recalled her husband's claim that she had ignored her parenting responsibilities to volunteer and attend workshops and seminars. Was this a pattern of behavior?

Once again, they went over Daddy's activities that day.

"Did Mr. Drew take any naps on that day?"

"No."

"Did he typically take naps?"

"No."

This flatly contradicted Mildred's statement that she had been told he was napping. Once again, I wondered if Pamela had been there when Mildred called or if another woman had answered the phone and made up the story about Daddy sleeping on the patio.

She'd taken Daddy on outings; she mentioned St Mary's Church— presumably when his friend Jonathan had seen him sitting alone in the car.

"When was the last time you were aware of Mr. Drew leaving the premises, the property at all?"

"We had gone to a farmers' market together."

"When was it that you took him to the farmers' market?"

'Well, it was a Saturday morning, that's when it happened, and –"

"It wasn't on July 21, was it?"

"I don't think so, no. I don't think so, no. It was not too much sooner than that. Does that make sense? No. I was only a time—it could have been the week before, maybe two weeks before."

• • •

Reading and rereading the transcript at home—our lawyer had sent it electronically—I was struck by Pamela's ambiguity as to whether she had taken Daddy out that day. A week after the disappearance she had emailed Matt and mentioned outings to St Mary's, Noble Horizons and "the Farmer's Market." In fact, her friend Karen Kisslinger had launched the Millerton, New York farmers' market on July 7, 2007; it ran every Saturday. Years later I saw photos of those July farmers' markets—but not of the launch. None of them showed Daddy or Pamela. So maybe the photographer hadn't seen them or they'd gone to the launch or perhaps the Kent farmers' market.

The first summer a woman had reported that on the evening of July 21 or 22 she had seen an aged man "sort of funny and bent over" walking south of Amenia on Route 22—between Nelson Hill Road and the Wassaic train station, on the opposite side of the road from the train station. The old man had turned "into a deep hollow area where there were trees," and she had lost sight of him. When she saw the flyer with Daddy's photo, she recognized him, she said.

Had Pamela taken him somewhere that day, lost him and, too ashamed to admit it, returned to his house to make brief alibi calls to her neighbors, pretending that everything was normal? As far as I know, that area along Route 22 has never been searched with canines.

Pamela had seen some police reports and mentioned the possible sighting at Noble Horizons, noting the woman's claim that the elderly man had said, "this is a loving home" and "lost."

"I thought that sounded possible," Pamela said.

She referred to the police report's claim about the woman's reputation for stretching the truth.

"I really would have put one of those psychics in touch with her, or put her in the lie detector, you know?" Odd that Pamela suggested a lie detector test for someone else, while refusing to take one herself.

"What is your current position about taking a polygraph test?"

"I'm not interested."

"If you were asked you would decline?"

"I would."

"Okay. I'm going to show you Exhibit 25 again." The lawyer read out Pamela's email to her town clerk sister.

"Do you see on the bottom where it says 'I just talked with the statistics, slash, investigators for Tom Drew and will be taking a five question YN polygraph test supposedly different from a lie detector test. This is supposed to alleviate family concerns, improve my integrity, oh joy.' What are you talking about there?"

"That—I think that's—a polygraph test is maybe different from a lie detector test."

"But you never followed through with that, correct?"

"No."

CHAPTER 10

Detective Warren had a long talk with our lawyer on April 18, almost three weeks after the second deposition. On the 21st he filed a report stating that "the deposition failed to produce any new leads." The next day he emailed me that another aerial search had produced nothing and that he had asked a forensic odontologist to review unidentified remains nationwide for matches.

Pamela didn't change her time frame, I emailed him that same day, but "she has now given a reason why she would not have wanted to call the police immediately in the event my father had left earlier." I was referring to her assertion that if she had been the one to report Daddy missing, her husband would have used it against her.

"I have not read the deposition in full yet and must reserve my opinion until I do so," he replied. "While I believe your hypothesis is likely, there does not appear to be much more that we can do." So he had written the deposition off as a source of leads without completely reading it.

"We were hoping it would give us some leverage," he later told me.

"What about the inconsistencies? The jacket that keeps changing? Her statements to the police said he was wearing a tan jacket, yet he obviously wasn't. Can't you follow that up?"

No reply.

"What about Mildred's call? Pamela seems to have no knowledge of it. Can't you call Mildred and check?"

Only silence.

Dismayed, deflated, I asked, "What else can I do?"

"You could depose Matt."

Despite my disappointment with his response, when I received Pamela's deposition and discovery items, there were new police files attached that helped me with my own investigation into Daddy's disappearance.

Our lawyer followed up the depositions by asking Pamela for a written hour-by-hour account of the day—to fill in the gaps in our knowledge of the day.

Pamela responded by hiring an attorney who advised her to *not* answer any more questions.

However, she brought her car—a 1996 Buick Century Sedan—to the police station. Desperate for any new information, after the deposition I had emailed Detective Warren asking the police to examine her car. From the outset, I had wondered whether Daddy's body had been put in her trunk and removed that first night.

I wasn't alone.

While helping me with a few odd jobs, Daddy's hunter friends discussed the case with me.

"That first night the police opened Matt's car trunk but let Pamela drive off without checking her car," I told them.

"There you go," said Woody.

I had been struck by Pamela's claim of hitting a deer and "damaging the rim above the tire." The police records show a dent at the top left front of the car—above and in front of the tire rim—as well as rust above the tire rim, but no apparent dent there. They swabbed the trunk for blood, with negative results that did not support my theory, the detective's report stated. Of course, if Daddy had simply collapsed, there'd presumably be skin cells in the trunk, but not necessarily blood. On the other hand, given that it was possible she had accidentally hit Daddy with her car, why didn't the detective examine the dent and the rust for blood?

In fact, it's not certain that the vehicle the police examined was the car she used when the disappearance was reported; the police hadn't recorded identifying details for the cars used by Matt or Pamela that day. And, after all, Daddy could have been driven off in someone else's car.

• • •

In the late spring Bettina learned about a decayed odor report just over the border in Massachusetts. Using maps, she pinpointed the location, called the woman who'd made the report and asked the Connecticut Canine Search and Rescue to check the new area.

Bettina couldn't accompany them: although her broken leg had knitted together, she needed a cane, and the terrain was too rough.

Back for the summer, I accompanied the team, struggling through the brambles along the conservation road.

"When was the last time a family member spoke to your father before he disappeared?" one of them, a retired marine, asked me as we walked.

"The police never asked me that! Bettina called him from Missouri on the Friday before he was reported missing, a few minutes after 6 pm. That would be … let's see … twenty-six hours before he was reported missing."

"Do you know if Matt and Pamela were having an affair? After all, an isolated spot … two lonely people."

"I … I just don't know … Anything's possible."

I remembered the used condom I had found at the bottom of the bathroom waste bin at the end of last summer.

Matt had been about to drive me to the train station. I had been doing last minute cleaning before leaving to catch the plane for England later that day.

I stared at the condom but was too embarrassed to ask him if it was his. Perhaps he had used it with his girlfriend. Or perhaps with Pamela. Or did Pamela have a boyfriend?

Should I keep it as evidence? Of course.

But I couldn't store it in the freezer, I reasoned, because Matt would find it, and he was going to be moving, anyway, and unplugging the freezer. I didn't know if I would have time to drop it at Troop B or if they'd even be interested in it.

So I threw it away, reassuring myself that it must have been for Matt and his girlfriend. And ever since I've rued my hasty decision.

Approaching the house, I could see Bettina leaning on her cane. She limped slowly towards us.

The searchers shook their heads; nothing.

Her face crumbled softly; she turned away.

That summer, as Barack Obama travelled across the country campaigning for the Presidency—*Yes we can*—I began my annual task of putting up flyers and contacting local papers to keep Daddy's disappearance in the public eye. I sat at the kitchen table inserting the flyers into plastic sleeves, glancing up to see a flock of wild turkeys parading on the lawn. Then I left with flyers and pushpins. At Taconic green a woman saw me pinning flyers on trees. She approached and said she had seen the old man people had mentioned the year before but hadn't come forward.

"I couldn't identify him. Sorry."

• • •

One year missing

However, new leads emerged. A local man named Pete—witness three—saw the new flyer and called the house. He told me that the year before his friend Jane had phoned him the afternoon of July 21, said Daddy was missing and asked if he could help search. He couldn't and still felt bad about it. He came to the house, we had a long conversation and he put me in touch with Jane—witness four.

Like Pamela, Jane had cared for Nelly's mother Noreen. According to Jane, Pamela's sister had phoned her *cell* number in the early afternoon of July 21 and said Tom Drew was missing and they needed help finding him. Jane was working at the Kent farmers' market and couldn't help, so she called Pete.

The following morning she saw Pamela, who confided she was afraid of going to jail. She said Pamela told her she had discovered Daddy missing in the morning and didn't know how long he had been gone. Jane had heard people say Pamela had been seen in Salisbury Pharmacy on the Saturday Daddy was reported missing. She said other locals knew Daddy had been missing earlier than reported but didn't want to come forward. No one wanted to rat Pamela out to the police; the locals looked out for each other. She also said Pamela had a boyfriend—a Torrington dentist, she thought, with whom Pamela had gone to high school. Did his name start with the letter D? She mentioned a name, but wasn't sure.

Jane was willing to wear a wire and talk to Pamela.

Detective Warren spoke to Jane and had her *cell* phone record checked. But the record showed no calls for that day, so her account was discredited.

He also checked Pete's two landlines. Pete claimed that in addition to Jane's call that day, he had received a call from Nelly, who was looking for Jane to help with her mother Noreen so she could help with the search. His phone records showed a call from Nelly's brother's house on the 22nd—the day after the disappearance. But they also showed two calls from Jane's *landline* on the day of the disappearance at 1:43 pm for 1.06 minutes, and again at 2:33 pm for 3.48 minutes—not long after the 1:17 and 1:22 pm calls from Daddy's house.

Was this just a coincidence? Couldn't one of Pamela's sisters or her daughter Dianna have called Jane on her *landline* and asked for help? Or perhaps Nelly went to Jane's place hoping to find her, but instead found her spare key and called Pete from there?

"Maybe she had a disposable cell," I appealed to Detective Warren. "Maybe the company didn't keep records. Or maybe she got confused about which phone she got the call on. After all, it was a year ago. Pete's phone records showed two calls from her *landline* on the 21st. Can't you check her *landline* record too? She may have received a call from Pamela's sister on that line. She told me she'd authorized the police to check both her phones."

Jane's account was persuasive. She thought Pamela had worked for Nelly early on July 21 and assumed she was hopping between both jobs trying to get paid for both. That was supported by Amelia's email to Pamela that Nelly had paid her for the hours she had worked that weekend.

Jane said Nelly kept a record book of the hours the caregivers worked.

But Detective Warren refused to budge.

• • •

The date of Matt's deposition was approaching. I had naively assumed he would want to help. Surely, he, too, needed closure. And he still called

Aunt Mildred. The year before I had been angry he hadn't immediately told me he was losing confidence in Pamela. But I didn't say anything. After all, I berated myself, I should've double-checked her references and interviewed her myself.

"You have to decide whether you're going to forgive Matt," Bettina told me. And I forgave him then and there. Initially, Pamela had worked occasional weekends for Daddy, trading off with the other part-time women. Only later on, in the spring and early summer, did she work alternate weekends. So Matt hadn't immediately realized she wasn't paying enough attention to Daddy. Once he did, he gave her a warning—about a week before the disappearance—expecting her to heed it if she wanted to keep her job.

All we wanted from Matt was as much detail as possible to piece together the day's events. Perhaps there was a detail forgotten from those twenty-six hours before Daddy was reported missing, or perhaps a small white lie, seemingly inconsequential at the time, that he wanted off his chest.

But Matt didn't want to help. We had to subpoena him. The date was rescheduled at his request. What was he playing at, still calling Mildred, when he wouldn't even answer questions? Didn't he know what the disappearance was doing to her—to all of us?

Did he have a grudge about his severance pay? Soon after the disappearance, Matt had come to me worrying about his situation. When he was hired we agreed he could stay in the house at no cost for three months after Daddy's death. I couldn't think straight; I had been working non-stop putting up flyers.

"Okay, I'll give you two months' severance pay, Matt."

"Well … that's something," he replied grudgingly.

But after my conversation with Karen Kisslinger, I couldn't give him another dime. By then, he had already received six weeks' severance pay. Nonetheless, he was angry when I stopped the last two weeks. He moved out in a rush, telling Bettina to come and collect Dandy.

Two years later I would access the email account Matt had used on Daddy's phone line—the email provider gave me a temporary password. When Matt moved out he deleted his emails. Most subsequent messages were junk mail. But I would spot an email from Pamela, written just a few days after her second deposition, asking him how much she had been paid—a surprising question given that she had been paid by check, and her bank had a record.

Her opening sentence—"I realize it's likely been helpful to not be in touch"—seemed to me like an admission of complicity, although perhaps she meant something else.

I would inform the police, who, as far as I know, would do nothing.

Now I emailed Detective Warren to ask him if he had any particular questions he would like us to ask Matt.

"Yes. If Matt could be asked again about when he left the house that day and whether or not he stayed there on the Friday night before," came his reply.

So the police apparently did have some uncertainty about Matt's movements.

• • •

The deposition finally took place in August at a law office in Pawling, New York. Bettina and I were present, but Matt didn't acknowledge us, nor we him. As the lawyer began asking questions, the stenographer taking notes, I sensed Matt's discomfort. He seemed to be distancing himself from Daddy. A month before the disappearance he had told me he was planning to stay until "the end," but he now stated:

"He was getting to the point where I felt he had to be put in a nursing home ... I was taking too much responsibility."

I sensed a forced emotional coldness. He seemed contemptuous of our ageing father. This was not the same man who'd purported to love Daddy.

Bettina fled the room.

I steeled myself; I needed to listen.

The lawyer asked about Daddy's physical condition in the last months before the disappearance.

"He wasn't able to walk around very much and he would go out just to the front of the yard and pick weeds or move ... he didn't really do too much, mostly picking weeds, moving pebbles around, or he'd sit and watch TV or sleep. He slept a lot."

That contradicted Pamela's claim.

"Would you please describe for me what his physical limitations were."

"We tried to walk up to the mailbox a few times within the months preceding his disappearance. By the time he got to the gates he would be very tired and he had to wait." Matt was referring to the two pillars marking Daddy's property.

"Did you at times encourage him to continue on for exercise?"

"No, because he was breathing hard and it didn't look like a good idea to have him move on."

"Describe for me how he walked; did he stand upright?"

"He limped and his balance wasn't good. We were not concerned with his wandering off. I was concerned about his balance and falling down. He was leaning on things when he walked out of the room, he would lean on things."

"And could you describe for me how that affected his walk?"

"It limited his speed and accuracy in walking. So it wasn't only balance—he was having problems with his leg and he would say my leg hurts. I remember him saying my leg hurts."

When asked which doors Daddy generally used, he again flatly contradicted Pamela's claim.

"Typically he would use the door to the garage or step out through the kitchen sliding doors ... I think it's especially true towards the last month."

"So he would use the garage door or the kitchen door?"

"The sliding door in the kitchen, yes, because it was summer and the glass door was open and he only had to open the screen door."

Yet on the critical matter of what time he left the house that day he was as vague as Pamela.

"Allison," he had told me the week after the disappearance, "I've gone over and over the events of that day in my mind, wondering if I could have done anything differently."

"Like what?"

"Built up his confidence more before I left."

I had genuinely believed him then.

Now, the lawyer asked him:

"Do you recall when you left the Drew residence?"

"I don't remember the exact time."

"Do you remember what part of the day it was?"

"Well, it was during the day."

"Had you already had breakfast with Mr. Drew?"

"I don't recall. I think Pamela—I don't recall."

"Okay. Do you know if you had lunch with Mr. Drew?"

"I did not have lunch with Mr. Drew, I don't believe I did."

"And how long a period of time did you two overlap from the time that, you know, she arrived and you left, approximately?"

"I'm thinking a half an hour, but I don't really recall."

"And in the course of the time that you did overlap did you see her interacting with Mr. Drew at all on that day?"

No, he replied, he did not.

But he did remember rushing to meet his girlfriend at the train station—a good forty minute drive from Daddy's house.

"And do you recall what time she was coming in?" the lawyer asked.

"No. Maybe 10 or 12. It must have been 10. That would be about right because I semi-recall being—you know, trying to get out of there."

"Because she was going to be waiting at the train station for you."

"That's right."

The lawyer pressed that point: "You believe you were leaving the house to meet a 10 o'clock train."

"I think so. I mean, that sounds about right."

"And Mr. Drew was in the den at the time you left?"

"Yes."

Where did he and his girlfriend Anna go, the lawyer asked?

"Well, we went to Millbrook."

"And that's where you spent the entire day?"

"You know, I couldn't tell you. I think we went to the park that day, I'm not sure. I don't recall what we did."

"You had testified that your best recollection was you left in the morning to meet [Anna] at a 10 o'clock train."

"That's what I recall."

"I'm going to show you one of the officer's investigative reports … Do you see here it says, 'On 7/21/07 at approximately 1500 hours [Matt] left the residence and picked up his girlfriend … so they could spend the day together' … So 1500 hours would be three in the afternoon rather than—(interrupted)

"Is it? Okay. Well"—(interrupted)

"10. Does that jog your memory that" (interrupted)

"Sort of. I was thinking—okay. I guess so, yeah. I wasn't—that's what I remembered. I couldn't remember ... Actually, that doesn't sound familiar."

"It doesn't sound familiar?"

"Evidently it is. I mean, it was a lot fresher information a year ago."

"Not to pry, but to try to get ... some better idea of when you might have actually left the house on that day, do you recall what you and [Anna] did on the day of the 21st?"

"As I said, I don't recall. We went to the restaurant, certainly ... Especially now, since it was evidently later, I think we probably just went to dinner."

When the deposition ended, Matt rose to leave. From the corner of my eye, I saw him cast a long, sideways glance at me. I stared down at the table. I couldn't bear to look him in the eyes, the man with whom I had expected to remain friends after Daddy's passing.

"Matt's changed his time frame," I told Detective Warren. "Please can you ask Anna what train she arrived on? Here's her number."

The detective dropped by Matt's apartment to ask about his changed time frame; he accepted at face value Matt's claim he had been nervous.

He also told me he had called Anna, although the police records I received don't indicate this. I spoke with him soon after. Anna stated she couldn't recall what train she took, the detective informed me, but she remembered that she and Pamela prayed together.

Was he was implying that I should be content with their prayers?

CHAPTER 11

Well, I wasn't satisfied with prayers. Historians are detectives—they uncover traces of events, find facts and interpret and reinterpret evidence by asking new questions. I was already using the skills I had developed uncovering new insights into South African and Algerian history to investigate Daddy's disappearance.

I wanted to trace the sixteen-minute call from Bridgeport, the Friday before Daddy was reported missing. I asked the police to request Daddy's phone records for the six months before the disappearance so that I could check whether the number had appeared before. They didn't, and since I couldn't access AT&T's official records, I did an online People Smart search. I traced the number to Rosemary, a woman in her 70s whom I visited. She told me it had been her number in 2007. She had two children, twins, the son deceased, and the daughter in her late 40s, living nearby. Rosemary told me she lived on her own and didn't know anyone in northwest Connecticut. I believed her. But couldn't a relative or a friend or neighbor have made the call?

I couldn't find anything linking Matt to the area, but to my surprise I discovered Pamela had lived there as a teenager. She had claimed to have graduated from Housatonic Valley Regional High School in Falls Village, and after Jane's tip about a dentist boyfriend, I perused its yearbooks. However, I couldn't find a record of Pamela and drew a blank on the hypothetical boyfriend. Subsequently, I learned Pamela had attended Wilbur Cross High School in New Haven, then transferred to and graduated from Roger Ludlowe High School in Fairfield—not far from Bridgeport.

How could anyone make a mistake about their high school?

Could Pamela have been working that Friday night? Could someone have called her and driven over? Of course, the police would have to confirm ownership of the Bridgeport number on that particular day with the phone company and then interview that owner.

I reported my findings to the police—to no avail.

Notwithstanding Matt's laconic litany of "can't recall" during the deposition, I remained convinced that emotionally he must need closure. After all, he had lived with Daddy for a year and a half and had always seemed very fond of him, despite his detachment now. Pamela's professions of not remembering, by contrast, were loquacious, weaving and meandering around each question. But regardless of their different styles, the result was the same—a dearth of detail about the day Daddy was reported missing.

I was teaching a course on the French-Algerian writer Albert Camus, whose fictionalized autobiography *The First Man* stresses memory's social underpinnings. "Poor people's memory is less nourished than that of the rich; it has fewer landmarks in space because they seldom leave the place where they live, and fewer reference points in time throughout lives that are grey and featureless." The heart remembers, he adds, but it "forgets sooner under the weight of fatigue … in order to bear up well one must not remember too much." Forgetting is a means of protection.

It reminded me of Daddy's remark about not wanting to remember. He had understood the need to avoid the pain of remembering.

I couldn't stop ruminating over why Pamela and Matt seemed to have such difficulty remembering that crucial day.

• • •

Insomnia became my nightly companion. That autumn, back in York, my only respite from Daddy's case was either to throw myself into other intellectual puzzles—piecing together the histories of South African and Algerian socialists—or, better yet, to ramble across the North Yorkshire moors with Jack. He had become warmer when I moved out; hoping that he still loved me, I proposed we try again. But he refused, so I settled on friendship, and he became my best friend, the one constant in my life. My feet heavy in their hiking boots, I tramped alongside Jack across fields of cows and sheep. Often, we ambled along the river bank to Kirkham Abbey and then around through the woods and fields. Occasionally, we hiked around the Hole of Horcum, scooped out, local lore claims, by Wade the Giant. My favorite walk was Spaunton Moor, near Lastingham, with its endless horizons. Sometimes we lay on the springy purple and magenta heather, our eyes on the sky, following the floating clouds. Those silences shared, those words exchanged as we gazed at the infinite shades of colors around us—for me that was love, and in that way I could forget my worries.

I was always seeking new approaches to Daddy's case. So I contacted Kelly Snyder, a retired police officer involved with an organization called *Find Me*, a non-profit group of psychics, retired law enforcement officers and canine search and rescue volunteers. Above all, I wanted to keep an open mind, and I accept that certain people are more sensitive to sensory data than others.

Kelly sent Daddy's photo to his psychic team members and got nineteen replies, which he forwarded to Detective Warren. Twelve psychics sensed that Daddy's remains were near or in water, and five felt he was in a ravine. They provided geographic coordinates. Six psychics believed the caregiver had lied to the police. One thought she had murdered Daddy and that his body had been removed and buried at a friend's junkyard/auto salvage business. Two others suggested he had been picked up and was still alive. Whether the detective ever considered the psychic reports, I don't know.

Bettina, in the meantime, relocated from Missouri to Salisbury with her animal entourage: Satin, a cooperative Dachshund who stood on her back legs hoping for treats; Ivy, a wraithlike rescue dog with an ear-shattering shriek; Daddy's Siamese Dandy and Odin Odinovich, a large seal point Siamese who transitioned smoothly from a cramped Russian flat to a Connecticut country estate. Poised and self-assured, Odin snoozed on the police vehicles, and on at least one occasion troopers had driven off only to find him napping in their car.

That fall Bettina broke her leg a second time. She had gone hiking with a Swedish visitor on the Appalachian Trail above Ravine Ridge

Road. They'd lost track of time. Darkness fell. She tripped and tumbled. In a scene unnervingly reminiscent of the initial hunt for Daddy, she lay in the pouring rain, only her head under cover, sucking water from her scarf fringe, while the rescue team searched in the pitch dark, the rain so intense they couldn't hear more than a few feet away. They finally found her around one am.

Over the next days I made some phone calls, organized her health insurance and found someone to move in with her while she recovered.

The evening of Obama's presidential inaugural ball I phoned Bettina, who was watching the ball live on TV.

"What's Michelle wearing?"

We were daughters of a fashion designer, after all.

Bettina described the one-shouldered white silk chiffon gown in intricate detail. The designer, Jason Wu, was only 26 years old.

New beginnings.

"Dear Attorney General Blumenthal," I began a letter-writing campaign, typing at my desk in York, Margo snoozing on my lap.

"I am writing about the disappearance of my father, Thomas Drew. My father's disappearance raises a point of fundamental importance: that every disappearance is a possible crime and that, accordingly, the last known place where the missing person was seen should be treated as a potential crime scene until the events leading to the disappearance can be established."

It was a detailed letter, summarizing the facts that we knew. I stressed the need to put aside stereotypes about dementia:

"People with dementia can also be the victim of gross neglect or crime. Their vulnerability makes them all the more susceptible to this, and popular presumptions and preconceptions about dementia can actually mislead the police from thinking in terms of a possible crime."

I sent similar letters to Chief State's Attorney Kevin Kane and Commissioner of the Department of Public Safety John Danaher. They were excruciating to write. It took weeks to work myself up to start writing and weeks to write them, mastering, suppressing my emotions with cold logic. Jack proofread them for me.

I spent my spring break in Salisbury with Bettina, slowly recovering from her accident.

Detective Warren had been transferred; frankly, I felt we needed a fresh pair of eyes. Enter Detective Chuck Riley. Bettina met him at the house after I had returned to York and thought he seemed smart and interested.

I had hope.

• • •

Pamela was again in the news.

Her teenage son, a gentle-faced boy with sad eyes, had leapt into a raging river to help two other boys who'd jumped in while celebrating the start of summer. A strong swimmer, he pushed the two boys towards a rock, then signaled 9-1-1 with his hands. One boy managed to climb out, the other was saved by a rescue worker. But rescuers couldn't reach Pamela's son. He was sucked under by the rushing currents. Heavy rains, record-high water levels, treacherous currents too dangerous even for professional divers. The search was suspended, the tragic events reported in the local and regional press.

The boy's body was found a week later.

Pamela's divorce was completed the day after the boy's death. The court records alleged a history of violence towards her minor children—which she denied. Pamela's husband Steve reported that she kept returning to the family home and ranting at the children. When the children tried "to end a lecture by leaving the room," she wouldn't let them. On one occasion she refused to leave their son's room "and would not let him out through the doorway." The boy "became so frustrated that he exited the second-story bedroom by climbing out of his window, jumping onto a side roof, and then jumping down to the ground outside." She threatened to send him to live with out-of-state relatives and even to ship him off to China.

Relations between Pamela and her son deteriorated to such an extent that the court decided Pamela could continue her parenting visits with her two minor girls, but her son would "have the option to attend visitation as he wishes." The husband was to retain the marital home. Pamela was to remove her possessions, but failed to do so. Her husband reported the boy was "currently using a very small bedroom because the Defendant is using the larger bedroom to store her personal belongings, despite having vacated the home." When asked to remove her possessions, she replied that if her son wanted more space, he could "find it by leaving the home and going to see his paternal grandparents."

Pamela's husband argued she was in contempt of court. But Pamela portrayed herself as the victim. She claimed he was denying her parenting time with her children. Over the past few years, she added, she had been "especially concerned by his numerous calls to police and DCF [Department of Children & Families] ... trying to prove that I am an unfit mother and following through with his threats to take the children from me permanently on a sole custody basis."

She denied the alleged abusive behavior towards her son. "While our son has expressed concerns about wanting to be away from me," she conceded, "we generally get along reasonably well." On that occasion the court did not find her in contempt.

But over the next few months the court's attitude hardened. Warning her that involving children in a divorce was considered child abuse, it substantially reduced her visitations with her children. Her husband sought relief from the $100 per week he was giving her since she wasn't providing much parenting nor looking for full-time work. He told the court that she "currently sees the children sporadically and for short periods of time, if at all." The court allowed her to have nightly calls with them between 8-9 pm and ordered her to pay for her own psychological examination. It warned her that another violation of the contact restrictions "could result in her incarceration."

Her husband claimed his son and oldest minor daughter "refused to see or speak to their mother," and that the minor children were "highly embarrassed by the Defendant's inappropriate behavior." Amazingly, she found employment as a babysitter for thirty hours per week. Had those parents not heard about Daddy's disappearance or the allegations Pamela was mistreating her own children? Who was giving her a reference? Didn't the court have anything to say about that? Evidently not.

Pamela's husband came home one afternoon to find his son "visibly upset." The court records reveal that the boy stated his mother "was saying bad things about the Plaintiff again, telling … [him] that he better 'keep an eye out' and 'keep notes' because his dad was likely to turn on him and yell at and abuse him."

The court accepted the husband's account, which was backed up by social workers who'd interviewed the children. Pamela was denied physical custody of her children, who were to continue living with their father.

"The Wife shall enjoy flexible and reasonable parenting time with the minor children as their schedules and wishes allow," the divorce judgment read. "The Wife shall participate in a mental health evaluation and follow any treatment deemed appropriate. It is important for the Wife to address her issues."

A local man who knew Pamela told me she had gone around Salisbury expressing outrage with the court decision to anyone willing to listen.

I pondered Pamela's portrayal of her relationship with Daddy. Just as she had acknowledged, in a limited manner, her son's desire for distance from her, she had acknowledged Daddy's desire for distance, his wish that she leave his home. If she had underplayed her alleged aggression towards her son, wasn't it conceivable she had done the same with regards to Daddy? I imagined the scenarios over and over again:

I want you to leave now.

No, it's not time.

This is my home. I don't want you here.

Had they scuffled? Did he fall?

Troop B detectives presumably knew of the divorce allegations and the court findings. Nonetheless, when it came to Daddy, their interview reports suggest a wholly unquestioning approach towards her claims. Indeed, I sensed a studied silence.

CHAPTER 12

Two years missing

Detective Riley and a colleague came to see me at Daddy's house. I had typed up a list of points that needed further investigation, and we sat at the kitchen table. Tall, middle-aged and confident, Detective Riley spoke casually, his eyes roaming restlessly around the kitchen. Then he snapped his head sharply, peering at me intently.

"People are saying, 'What goes around, comes around.'" He was referring to Pamela's son.

"I've heard that, but I don't agree. The boy's death was a tragedy."

We discussed my points at length.

Surprisingly, Detective Riley had read Kelly Snyder's report and referred to the claim of one psychic that Daddy's body had been buried at the junkyard/auto salvage business of the caregiver's friend. He mentioned that the witness who lived next door to one of Pamela's relatives had a bunch of cars on his property. I was intrigued by this. It indicated imagination and lateral thinking. Then, to my delight, he added,

"I think this case *can go* somewhere. I've had cases I know can't go anywhere because all the leads have been exhausted. I have a pile of them on my desk. But there are lots of leads here that haven't been pursued."

I gave him the 2007 train schedule I had picked up in Grand Central so he could check Anna's possible arrival times, as well as Daddy's check registers to copy for a record of the hours worked by the part-time employees. I also gave him additional items with Daddy's DNA.

Detective Riley said he had scheduled a meeting with Pamela some months earlier, but she canceled the morning of the interview on her attorney's advice. He had also tried, unsuccessfully, to contact Matt—although later I googled and found him easily.

I gave him two weeks before calling to check on his progress.

"Did you check Jane's landline record and look into the Bridgeport call?" I asked, hopefully.

"My supervisor told me not to work the case unless I had nothing else to do," he replied. I was dismayed. From the brief synopsis I later found in the case file, he had evidently decided to follow Detective Warren's line of enquiry, which overlooked Jane's landline calls to Pete. Soon after I drove Daddy's car to the station and asked them to examine it forensically, but Detective Riley insisted it was too late to find evidence.

Things were at a standstill.

• • •

In July 1999, elderly James Garris disappeared from a Litchfield assisted living facility, five days after his family had relocated him from his Granby home. The case was reported in the *Hartford Courant* and the *Register Citizen*. Police dogs tracked his scent to a nearby Stop & Shop parking lot. That same morning the police received a report of an elderly man walking at the White Memorial Conservation Center—a popular rambling spot for people of all ages. They searched the White Memorial woods for days—even after two witnesses acquainted with Garris reported speaking to him at his local Granby store on the very morning he disappeared. Very likely Garris got a lift from the Stop & Shop to the Granby store while the police were searching the White Memorial woods. Although the police searched the area around his Granby house, they apparently didn't undertake a canine search from his local Granby store. Just as they were now doing with Daddy, they evidently discounted witnesses and used the excuse of dementia and its associations of *wandering* to pursue one line of enquiry only.

• • •

I flew to South Africa for a Johannesburg conference and the paperback launch of my Bunting biography in early September 2009. I visited Cape Town, where a former student, a South African Communist Party member, invited me to talk about Bunting at his local communist party branch meeting. An MP at the branch meeting invited me to address the

African National Congress Caucus at the Old Assembly Chamber in the South African Parliament on Bunting's life and legacy. It was fifteen years since the 1994 democratic transition; many younger MPs hadn't been in the liberation struggle and didn't know its history. I had only jeans and a sweater I had bought in Quebec City, but luckily I had packed a silk scarf, which I draped around my neck. Then off to Durban for another launch before returning to York. Exciting, but as I moved between the three continents, I felt increasingly isolated, as if I belonged nowhere.

My new approach to Daddy's case was to contact my elected representatives. I left a message for State Representative Roberta Willis who lived locally and had known Daddy. She was preparing a Silver Alert bill modeled after the Amber Alert system for missing children, which broadcast an emergency alert on radio and television as soon as a child was reported missing. Her website mentioned Daddy's case, stating, to my dismay, that Daddy had walked off. The next day her aide called me back.

"Representative Willis wants to know your view on the Silver Alert bill."

"I support it, but I doubt it's relevant to my father's case." I explained that aside from the canine scent partway up the conservation road, there was no physical evidence he had left the house on foot, but that the circumstantial evidence that he didn't walk away was overwhelming.

I emailed Representative Willis:

"I thought you might want to be updated on my father's case, particularly as you mentioned his and my names on your web site ... this article implies that my father vanished as a result of walking away. To date no evidence has been found to support that claim."

Representative Willis removed our names from her website, but I never heard back from her.

It was a blow, but I moved on, excited to learn that Connecticut Congressman Chris Murphy was preparing legislation on missing persons. What a relief to find an experienced politician who shared my concerns. His Help Find the Missing Act was dubbed "Billy's Law" after thirty-one-year-old Waterbury resident Billy Smolinski, who'd gone missing in August 2004. The case was widely reported in the Connecticut press and spotlighted in an August 2014 *Newsweek* article on the "silent mass disaster" of missing persons. The proposed legislation would combine the publicly-accessible National Missing and Unidentified Person System database (NamUs) with the FBI's National Crime Information Center (NCIC) database, thus simplifying how state and federal officials kept track of missing persons. This would help keep family members in the loop.

In January 2010 Billy's mom Jan Smolinski testified in support of "Billy's Law" at a House of Representatives subcommittee. As she explained,

"Looking for your missing loved one becomes a full time job … You have to continually hound the police, knock on doors, make phone calls, visit the media, make fliers, create Web sites … the connected NCIC-NamUs database that the legislation creates increases the chances of finding answers."

Surely, Congressman Murphy would want to meet the daughter of his missing constituent. I got an appointment with his aide. She was cordial but said Congressman Murphy had too many demands on his time to meet me. She contacted the police on my behalf, relaying back their assurances they'd done everything possible to find Daddy.

No, I replied:

"They still have not checked all the phone records from the day my father was reported missing, nor certainly as late as the past two or three weeks, have they checked relevant cell records, emails, nor the alibi of the live-in companion."

Congressional representatives represent their constituencies at the national level. The state police don't fall under their remit, and perhaps there was little else Congressman Murphy's office could do. I tried more than once to get an appointment with the congressman. That, despite his concern with missing persons legislation, he was invariably too busy to meet me was yet another blow.

Enter Lieutenant Daniel Leonard. Tall, serious, fortyish, he seemed to have risen rapidly up the ranks. He and Sergeant Sam Sierra came out to the house. We sat around the kitchen table. Sierra, perhaps a few years younger than Leonard, seemed nervous, as if under scrutiny.

"What's Pamela like? How old is she?" Lieutenant Leonard asked him.

Sergeant Sierra inhaled.

In that moment I realized Sergeant Sierra was very likely the supervisor Detective Riley had mentioned when I called him and the link between all the detectives who'd worked on the case.

"Oh … late 40s," he replied.

We went outside onto the back patio and down to the lawn.

"He could be anywhere," Sergeant Sierra said, gesturing with his arm.

"That's not true," I said, tired of being acquiescent and fed up with accepting the assertions and opinions of these uniformed men as the truth.

"Lots of possibilities have already been eliminated through searches, through probability over time and because of my father's physical condition."

Lieutenant Leonard, seemingly lost in thought, gazed across Daddy's back yard at the trees beyond and murmured, almost to himself:

"They're both lying. If he'd walked off, we would have found him within 24 … 48 hours."

Their walkie-talkies crackled; they had to leave.

Nonetheless, I was hopeful that day.

I was still hopeful when I met with Lieutenant Leonard at Troop B barracks two weeks later. I noticed that a one-way glass barrier had been installed at the counter in the waiting area so that the public could no longer see the people working behind the counter. So now the police needed privacy and protection from the public? In Litchfield County of all places? I had barely sat down when a trooper came to escort me to the lieutenant's office.

"Morning." We chatted for a minute or two about England. He had taken his family there, he said, pointing to a photo of his wife and son in front of the Tower of London. Then, flipping through a very thick loose-leaf binder containing Daddy's case records, Lieutenant Leonard assured me that the police had followed up all the leads. I held my tongue, needing to be tactful.

"I read Matt's deposition and, yes," he conceded, "his vagueness about the day in question seems odd. I would have thought that day would be stuck in his mind forever. If it had been me, I would have gone over the events repeatedly." He sure wished he could bring Pamela in for a polygraph, he added.

Could I persuade him to interview Pamela's daughter Dianna, request Jane's landline record and check out the Bridgeport call? Swiftly, I made my case and genuinely believed I had convinced him.

• • •

Three years missing

Lieutenant Leonard's arrival briefly energized the investigation.

Detective Riley drove to Pamela's home where he found her very willing to talk about her personal problems—her deceased son, her failed marriage. But she would have to check with her attorney before talking about Daddy, she told him.

I appealed once more to Lieutenant Leonard.

"If your elderly relative went missing and after three years the police had still not checked out all the phone calls to and from his house, what would you think?" I emailed. "The only reason anyone thinks my father left by foot is because a woman who refuses to take a polygraph claims that he left on foot at 7:20 pm wearing a jacket whose color she could not recall, when no jacket was ever found missing."

Always trying to keep several irons in the fire, I turned again to the media. A *Litchfield County Times* reporter had recently reviewed Michael Dooling's *Clueless in New England,* and mentioned Daddy's case. I wrote to thank him, and he proposed writing an update on Daddy's case. He came out to the house to look around. Young, dark-haired and sharp, he asked all the right questions.

His article was headlined "Lack of Answers in Salisbury Case."

Another reporter rang to discuss Daddy's story.

"There was a time when the resident trooper was an avuncular local guy who genuinely wanted to be helpful. No more," he remarked. "They don't like being shown up."

"They're state employees, only interested in their pensions," he added.

It was what I had dreaded.

"There was another missing person case—a woman. The police found her car and drove it to the Troop B lot. But it was 4 pm on a Friday. They wanted to go home, so they didn't pop the trunk. When they finally opened it on Monday morning, they found her body." But not wanting to jeopardize his source, he never reported the episode. I've often wondered whether she was already dead when they found the car or whether she died over the weekend.

The Connecticut Canine Search and Rescue still carried out periodic searches for Daddy. Every year since the disappearance their dogs had been giving the signal—Bartl's alert—for a "decayed human scent" at 042° 02' 57.09" N x 073° 24' 39.52" W, just over the boundary of Daddy's property, not far from the conservation road where the search dogs had picked up Daddy's scent, but beyond the Ravinehurst bridge. They duly informed the police, but I didn't learn about this until three years after the disappearance, when Bettina and I finally secured more material from the police file using the Freedom of Information Act.

Freedom of Information has two tiers. The first applies to the federal or executive branch government agencies and was passed in 1966. It was established to counter the state secrecy of the Cold War era by promoting government transparency and strengthening the constitutional rights of citizens. Because government agencies were poor at disclosing information, in 1974—following Richard Nixon's imperial presidency and the Watergate scandal—Congress gave the Freedom of Information Act greater power to force government agencies to comply.

Individual states also have Freedom of Information Acts. Our requests fell under Connecticut's, passed in 1975. According to Connecticut law, public agency meetings must be open and their records available for "prompt" disclosure to and inspection by the public—subject to exemptions, not surprisingly. For example, the police were not required to send full interviews but, rather, interview summaries. These were nonetheless helpful.

Bettina and I began writing directly to the state police Legal Affairs Department. The files we received were in haphazard order and often duplicates of the earlier investigation. To me this suggested poor record-keeping. Yet, when I had met with Lieutenant Leonard in his office, his file was neatly organized in a loose-leaf binder with colored tabs marking the different sections.

I now emailed Lieutenant Leonard.

"Since the dogs keep going back to the same site, surely there is sufficient probable cause to dig up this area, which is mainly covered with brambles."

No reply.

• • •

That summer, a research trip to Paris—I was working in earnest on my Algeria book—then back to York to write up my Paris notes. Whenever I sat in the garden with a cup of tea, Margo would rouse herself from her naps between the lavender and catmint, and we would sit side by side on the low brick wall, her face lifted to the sky, the breeze ruffling her long hair. Some Sundays Jack and I wandered in the countryside or just meandered in the car till we found a place to eat, the Ramblers' Rest in Millington, being a favorite. I was happy. I felt normal.

In the fall, needing to reach out to someone knowledgeable about missing persons cases, I contacted Michael Dooling. He had read about the case, and when I returned to Salisbury late that year he visited, bringing a copy of his book. Early sixties, tall, bewhiskered and bespectacled, he asked lots of questions, and together we tramped along the conservation road. Later I sent him copies of the police files and depositions.

Our neighbor Otto, still upset by Daddy's disappearance, expounded at length about the influence of town clerks and claimed that the police had never interviewed him. Pamela had knocked on his door a day or so after the disappearance, ranting about her personal problems, but seemingly oblivious to Daddy's vanishing and the possibility that he might still be alive, if he had left on foot.

"Did Tom vaporize?" he asked in exacerbation. "And what about the boyfriend?" He presumed she must have had one.

Jane, too, had cautioned me about town clerks.

"Susan's friends work behind the counter at Troop B," she had told me before the one-way glass barrier had been erected. "They saw me come in and phoned her." Was I too worried about this problem? Perhaps even paranoid?

I emailed State Senator Andrew Roraback, complaining about the inefficiency of the investigation and the potential conflicts of interest in the tiny Northwest corner towns.

"Your instincts are right on," State Senator Roraback replied. "In the small towns of NW Ct. we all seem to know one another."

We spoke on the phone.

"I'm worried the police have fallen back on stereotypes about dementia in order to avoid following up leads into my father's disappearance. Given the intensity of the searches, my father's frailty and the failure of the canines to find any physical evidence, I believe he was removed by car."

"Why would someone do that?" asked the Senator.

"Panic? Maybe there was an accident, and the person was afraid of being blamed."

"You mean maybe he fell in the shower?"

"It's perfectly possible he fell. People have pointed out that the woman who worked for my father that day is the sister of a local town clerk. They've suggested that small-town politics are blocking the investigation."

"I know the town clerk," he swiftly replied. "She's a very nice lady."

"Maybe it's easier for the police to claim that my father walked away rather than to investigate. I can't find out what's going on."

"I'll talk to the police and get back to you."

I never heard back.

CHAPTER 13

"Daughter of Missing Man in Salisbury is Persisting" ran the January 1, 2011 *Litchfield County Times* headline. Lieutenant Leonard, irritated, mentioned the article when I spoke to him soon after. Painfully disappointed with my elected representatives, I had refocused on the media. But each time I called a journalist I would have to repeat the whole story, telling, retelling the complicated tale—would it never end? I had no respite.

But I had no choice.

By now my case file was swollen with canine searches, depositions and jumbled-up police reports. Back in York, I would sit on the floor in my home office, legs crossed, surrounded by the documents, searching for patterns, for some detail I had overlooked. I separated the documents into piles, first chronologically, then thematically, then reassembled them and started over again. The papers seemed to shift and shuffle of their own accord, swarming around me. I had to get them off the floor.

Margo, sensing my distress, pressed herself against me, circling me, wrapping me in her affection.

• • •

Maintaining Daddy's house was costly. Bettina had moved to Georgia, but she and I needed to spend time at the house to continue our search. The previous summer we had listed the house as a seasonal rental with Sabrina, who ran a local real estate office. Judging by her wardrobe, she wasn't well-to-do, but she dressed in that relaxed *Land's End* style popular with New Englanders, and her highlighted hair was stylishly cut. With her breezy, easy-going attitude and warm smile, she had flattered us, pricing the furnished four-bedroom house at $30,000 for three months.

But in February, with no takers, Sabrina proposed she rent the house for herself, her granddaughter and their dog and cat at $900 per month.

"Both of you would be most welcome to come and stay at the house and invite guests when your time permits," she added.

We agreed on $1,000 plus utilities. After some procrastination, Sabrina drafted and signed the lease, which had a clause allowing Bettina and me to visit and occupy our bedrooms; Sabrina had highlighted the clause in red ink when she sent us the lease to review. Bettina had a sixth sense about Sabrina's delay, but, naively, I thought she had just been busy. We weren't present to make an inventory before Sabrina moved in, but I didn't anticipate any problems; after all, she was a well-known local business woman. I loved the house and wanted to spend more time there when I retired, so I hoped to make new friends.

Sabrina mentioned Daddy's case.

"Pamela? She's something else," she said, rolling her eyes as she offered her opinion.

"Why do you say that?"

"A good friend of mine knows the family and can tell you plenty. I showed her in-laws' house when it was on the market. In fact, I remember your phone number because Pamela called my office from your home seeing if she could buy their house on a credit card. I have lots of contacts and can help you find out more about her."

I was hooked.

• • •

That May the state police used dogs to search Hautboy Hill Farm in Cornwall. Michael Dooling had been intrigued by Pamela's dream of finding Daddy's skeleton behind a dresser with high legs. He pointed out that hautboy—in French, literally, high wood—could be construed as highboy, a dresser with high legs. Had this been Pamela's unconscious way of indicating where Daddy's body had been hidden? Pamela evidently knew the farm; her late son had been friends with the owner's son. The road leading to a private, wooded area behind the farm had very little traffic, and one could easily enter unseen, despite the chains blocking the entrances.

Later, when I once again returned, Michael and I met at the Goshenette, a cute diner in Goshen, Connecticut and a convenient halfway meeting point. We mulled over the Hautboy Hill Farm hypothesis. The conversation turned to Pamela's claims about hitting a deer.

"Is she trying to create a reason for the damage to her car? Was it really a deer that caused the damage?" Michael mused.

His thoughts unfurled.

"Did you notice that in the deposition she mentioned the possibility of your father being hit by a car?" Wasn't it possible, he speculated, that Pamela was away part of the day and that when she came back, perhaps rushing, she accidentally hit him with the car. Maybe he was standing in the driveway.

Yes, I replied. I thought it bizarre that she of all people was suggesting criminal behavior. But it was also possible that her car hit one of the chains across the Hautboy Hill Farm entrances.

The police and canine handlers entered the farm through the southern entrance off Route 43. They canvassed the area south toward the farm, but not, as far as I know, the area north to the intersection of routes 63 and 43. That same afternoon the police investigated Bartl's alert with a police dog and a metal detector. Unlike the previous positive canine alerts, however, the dog didn't give the signal for a decayed human scent.

The Hautboy Hill Farm search was covered in the *Litchfield County Times* and the *Republican-American*. On May 10 the *Republican-American* published an article titled "Police search farm for clues in Salisbury man's disappearance." The online article was followed by voluminous comments; curious, I scrolled down to read them.

Someone dubbing himself "Local man" had written:

"I recall seeing him, and the man could barely walk unassisted ... he could not have walked even a short distance from his door on the night that he is alleged to have disappeared."

What followed was in turn astonishing and disturbing. Since her divorce, Pamela had been drifting around the northwest corner: several rentals in Sharon and Salisbury and periodic stays with one of her brothers in Falls Village. A series of rambling comments by "Butterflyer"—some thirty-six single-spaced pages in all—referred to Pamela in the third person and rebutted any suggestion she had been less than completely honest. Later, reading the police records, I would learn that Pamela acknowledged having written these comments.

"There may have been conflicting reports regarding what [Pamela] said to someone on the phone, but she has never indicated that Tom Drew was not in his home with her or in the immediate vicinity of his home with her until the evening when he said he wanted to go out," Butterflyer wrote. "The aftermath of Tom Drew going missing involved a fairly high degree of tension, and while some reasonable concerns for clarity were requested, all of that would have been given voluntarily."

She expanded:

"There could be small chance that after wandering, and reportedly seen by someone, Tom Drew was hurt accidently or intentionally by someone who was drunk or of ill-intent. He possibly could then have been taken to another location." But, she maintained, "that seems highly unlikely given the short time he was unaccounted for before the search was underway."

Local gal responded:

"People are responsible for what goes on during their own work shift … what happened that day?"

Local man added:

"The newspaper article clearly states that Mr. Drew's caretaker at the time of his disappearance was watching a movie on television, at the exact time that he is alleged to have walked out of his door and subsequently disappeared. Someone that is paid to do a job that involves caring for a frail elderly man, should not be watching television and ignoring the man's needs."

Local gal pressed the point:

"You said earlier that your friend knew Mr Drew 'got weaker' with 'more dementia.' Then why did she remain watching TV when she claims he expressed the desire to go outside?"

Butterflyer responded suggestively:

"No one intentionally wanted any harm to come to Tom Drew." Was she implying that something *unintentional* happened, I mused?

Local man queried:

"How could someone who is being paid to care for a frail elderly man, allow that man to wander off and disappear while she was watching television, and then try to avoid taking responsibility?"

Friend of Tom's chimed in:

"His live-in companion gave the woman a warning the week before because she had been ignoring Tom. Quite clearly she chose to disregard the warning."

"She told him she would be out in a few minutes," Butterflyer replied defensively. This was a new claim: As far as I knew, Pamela had never said this, either in the police statements nor the deposition.

Someone styling themselves "Seeking a higher plane" joined the conversation:

"I wonder if this gentleman could have wandered into a road and met with a tragic accident and someone became scared and hid his body."

Local man speculated:

"Could he have been hit by a car on the private road that leads from his house to the main road?"

Butterflyer meandered around the subject:

"When people consider that many are lost at sea, in floods or earthquakes … we can consider we may not always have a certain answer. If there were foul play after he left the property, that would have been highly unlikely it seems, given the generally quiet nature of these towns."

Local gal had the last word:

"A frail elderly man who needed oxygen and walked very slowly vanished into thin air under your friend's watch. Do you think something happened at the house that day? Perhaps an accident?"

CHAPTER 14

"Girls, introduce yourselves."

I had contacted more reporters, hoping to persuade them to interview the four witnesses. One of them was planning an article about Daddy's case, so I flew back for a month that summer. Sabrina had come to pick me up at the train station, but dashed out of the car just as I was getting in.

Two very pretty girls, about twelve or thirteen, one white, one black, sat in the back. One girl had a dare in her eyes. The other sat with downcast eyes. I studied the girl with downcast eyes.

"Are you Sabrina's granddaughter?" I asked her.

She lifted her eyes and nodded.

We arrived at the house. I got my suitcase, and headed towards the front path to the house, the gravel crunching under my case's wheels.

"Oh, by the way," Sabrina said, "there was a problem with the entrance hall floor. I asked some workers to repair the cracked tile, but they took out the entire floor."

I couldn't fathom what she meant until I saw the front entrance. Broken marble tiles were scattered all over the steps. I opened the door. The marble floor had been removed, leaving plywood. I stood there, aghast, before touring the house. To my dismay, she had also stripped the dining room and bathroom wallpaper and repainted those rooms—the lease be damned.

Furious, I called the painter whose workers had destroyed the marble floor. He agreed to cover the cost of a new marble floor. In shock, I resolved to put the incident behind me.

I had brought some Blue Grass cologne as a gift and, on autopilot, not having fully processed the events, that evening I gave it to Sabrina.

She hadn't unpacked, I noticed with surprise, and she seemed to be struggling financially with the lawn mowing, so I paid it that month, and on my last night took Sabrina, her granddaughter and the girl's friend out to dinner.

But I was so consumed with Daddy's case that after ordering the new marble and overseeing the floor's installation I spent the rest of the trip meeting with police and reporters, desperate to move the case forward before returning to York to teach.

Daddy's case was reallocated to Detective Trevor Quinn, a bland-looking thirtyish investigator who conveyed the impression of being totally uninterested in the matter. Pamela had called him after the Hautboy Hill Farm media attention to tell her side of the story. They scheduled an appointment but she canceled that very morning on her attorney's advice.

I repeatedly tried to convince the police to request Jane's landline and Matt's internet records for the day in question. I believed that Matt's emails could help fill in the time frame. Detective Quinn contacted AT&T about the internet record and was informed that deleted emails weren't recoverable. But Yahoo, the service provider, told me that even deleted emails were recoverable. I relayed the information to the detective, to no avail.

Detective Quinn conducted a few phone interviews; the interviewees needn't worry they would be caught off guard or their expressions might give them away if he arrived at their homes unexpectedly. He phoned Ronnie, whose memory had improved with time: she was now certain Matt had called her late on the morning of the disappearance. He called Nelly about Jane's claims that Pamela had worked for her the day of the disappearance and that Nelly had kept a record book. Apparently, this was the first time Nelly was interviewed. She confirmed she had employed Pamela, but couldn't specify dates. Her mother had died in 2010, and "all of the diaries, journals, and all other paperwork concerning her care were destroyed." So Jane's claim of a record book—overlooked by the previous detectives—was finally confirmed, but the lead this offered vanished when it was destroyed.

The detective also phoned Matt's girlfriend Anna, who now recalled having arrived at the Wassaic, NY station around 6 pm—like Ronnie, her memory improved with time. She and Matt had driven to Millbrook, New York, had dinner and arrived back at Daddy's around 7:30 pm.

The detective seemed satisfied.

I went online and double-checked.

I found that the distance from Wassaic to Millbrook was nine to twelve miles and 17-19 minutes by car. They would have arrived at Millbrook about 6:20 pm. The shortest distance from Millbrook to Daddy's house was 29.5 miles and 43 minutes, depending on traffic. To arrive back at Daddy's around 7:30 pm, they would have had to leave Millbrook at 6:45 pm. That left 25 minutes to order, wait for the food to arrive, eat dinner and pay the bill. Why drive to Millbrook for such a rushed meal when they could have eaten in Millerton *en route* to the house?

When pressed, Detective Quinn shrugged.

• • •

Four years missing

The *Sunday Republican* published a long article to mark the fourth anniversary of Daddy's disappearance. The article noted Daddy's frail condition and remarked that neither Daddy's nor Pamela's car had been searched at the time of the disappearance. This was followed on July 29 by my letter to the editor, which the paper had titled "Real Story of Missing Salisbury Man has yet to be told." "We don't have a verified, factual time frame for July 20 and 21," I wrote. "When I arrived at the house on July 24, I discovered that the Caller ID record for July 21 and July 22 had been deleted."

When I met Lieutenant Leonard at the station before I returned to England, he was brusque, annoyed. No matter how diplomatic I tried to be towards the police, my public criticism was clear.

I flew to Algeria where I had arranged to interview people who'd been in the Algerian Communist Party and the FLN—National Liberation Front—during the war of independence. Algeria's aspirations for democracy had been thwarted by a one-party state, a military coup and civil war. Since then it had adopted a limited multi-party system, but the military still wielded power behind the scenes. Those I interviewed were eager to talk. Algerians, I discovered, had an elegant way of describing their state: *le pouvoir*—power.

From Algiers I flew south to Ghardaïa, where I draped a long scarf over my head and conducted several interviews, then hired a driver to take me to Algiers, Oran, Tlemcen, back to Algiers and on to Constantine, stopping at the Roman ruins at Tipaza, which Camus so loved.

But Salisbury wouldn't leave me in peace.

Soon after my arrival in Algeria I learned that Hurricane Irene, reduced to a tropical storm, had hit northwest Connecticut. On the remote chance that Daddy's remains were on or near the property, I wondered if the storm might churn them up. Instead, the stream surged, sweeping away the footbridge with the plaque honoring the hunters who'd built it—razing Daddy's past—gushing across the front lawn, flooding the basement. By email I arranged to have the basement pumped, cleaned and sanitized.

Then, in the small back room of the Algiers bookstore *El Ijtihad*, I sat and listened to veterans of the armed struggle, men and women, recount the torture they'd suffered in their efforts to free their country from colonialism.

Back in York, I discovered Sabrina hadn't paid her rent. I emailed her—no response. I called repeatedly—and got the answering machine. Eventually she wrote to say that the house was uninhabitable. When I tried to arrange for a local man to check the house, she refused him entry. I called her office staff and was told she was out. I called the real estate firm to which she was affiliated.

No help.

The summer's publicity about Daddy's case had drawn a belated response from the state police. Three detectives drove to Daddy's house in November to examine his car for blood—with negative results. A week later, Detectives Warren and Quinn used a rotary wing aircraft to conduct an aerial search of the swampy area northeast of the house, taking digital photos with a video camera. Detective Warren suggested Daddy had wandered a long way through dense thickets, brambles and woods to the swampy area and been sucked in—even though animals who died there lay on the surface and attracted vultures. The summer evenings were thick with mosquitos and horse flies, which Daddy hated. Leaving aside his physical frailty, why would he have slogged into a swamp, to be consumed by insects? The claim wasn't credible, particularly when there'd been no scent heading towards the swamp, no footprints, no broken brambles, no flattened reeds and no vultures circling overhead.

Did evidence—or its absence—mean nothing when it came to someone with dementia?

The area was contaminated due to the multitude of searches, countered Detective Warren. But didn't he recall that hours before those searches began, the only scent picked up that first night was across the back yard and up the conservation road? Didn't he know that early on Daddy's hunter friends had trudged into the swamp well beyond any tracks, and that neither they nor any other people had seen vultures? And hadn't he considered that someone might have dragged a piece of Daddy's clothing to leave a scent—as searchers had suggested several months after the disappearance?

• • •

Teaching at the university, my mind was now consumed not just with Daddy's case, but with anxiety over the house. The house symbolized Daddy, and with Daddy missing, I couldn't bear the idea of losing his possessions and the artwork my parents had so lovingly created.

I hired a Torrington attorney who suggested I ask the Salisbury resident trooper to accompany a local person acting on my behalf to check Sabrina's claims. The trooper refused, saying the police didn't get involved in civil matters. He sent an extract of the state statute on landlord access to rentals. This I forwarded to my attorney who sent me the complete statute, noting that both the statute and the lease gave me access to the property to conduct repairs and that my lease gave me the right to visit and occupy a spare bedroom. I sent this information to the police.

"This matter is a civil matter which your attorney can address," the trooper wrote back.

I called my lawyer.

"I want to make sure I'll be following the law and won't be arrested."

"There's a difference between what the police can do and what they can do legally," he replied.

To me this sounded like a truism.

Immediately after our conversation he emailed: "Your lease contains a provision allowing you to visit the property when you are here, and therefore, I see no legal reason prohibiting you from entering the property in accordance with your lease."

The detectives who'd examined Daddy's car thought the house looked deserted. "Detective [Quinn] advised me that the tenant had appeared to move out and that Allison Drew had legal rights to this property and residence," reported Detective Kate King on December 6. And on the 11th Otto emailed me that he had checked the house and "found no one at home and no evidence in the snow that anyone had come or gone."

Assured of my legal right to enter my home, and hoping, as Detective King had reported, that Sabrina had left, at the end of the academic term I returned to Salisbury. But I was thinking only of the law. I forgot about power—until then, state power had been an abstraction I studied in other countries, not my own.

By then I had lost all hope that anyone at Troop B would request the phone and internet records that might help to clarify the time frame around Daddy's disappearance. I wrote to forensic scientist Dr Henry C. Lee, asking him to review the case. No reply. I wrote to Police Commissioner Reuben Bradford and State's Attorney for the Litchfield Judicial District David Shepack:

"The investigation into my father's disappearance has been conducted according to generalizations about a particular category of people rather than according to the evidence. The physical evidence in the house was never collected and is thus lost … If my father is to be found and the events of that day revealed, the case will have to be removed from Troop B and handled by an independent investigator."

No reply.

Twelve days before Christmas, I learned that the state police had changed their mind about intervening in a civil matter.

CHAPTER 15

Approaching the house, I noticed two window shutters askew, one banging lightly against the wall. Tropical storm Irene had snapped off limbs and branches, which were strewn across the lawn. The storm's wrath had even damaged the hefty tree on the far right whose biggest branch lay on the ground, the swing it once held entangled in its own ropes. Sharp winds had scattered rusty-looking leaves across the lawn and ensnared them in the hedges, whose gnarled branches reached upwards. I stepped out of the car door. Cold nipped my face as I inhaled the scent of pine. A stag with ornate antlers, motionless on the back lawn, momentarily distracted me from my worries.

My lawyer had advised me to bring a witness. Jocelyn pulled up, closely followed by my new realtor Robert, who'd come to take photographs. We walked up the path to the front door, the gravel crunching underfoot.

We entered the house. I tapped in the code, but the alarm shrilled. As I had expected, Sabrina had changed the code without telling me.

The air inside was very still, as if it had been undisturbed for some time. The heat was set at 50 degrees Fahrenheit; the sink was filled with dirty dishes.

To my relief, however, the house was perfectly inhabitable, our furniture in place, and Maufra's *Sacré-Coeur* still there on the wall.

In Connecticut law, "surrounding circumstances" are key in determining whether tenants have left.

"The most persuasive is that the tenants have removed all or substantially all of their possessions," states the *Landlord/Tenant Disputes Police Training Manual*.

Sabrina's dish drain and her cat, dog, pet bowls and kitty litter box were gone, along with most of her possessions. Only a few items did not belong to my family: two pieces of pine furniture, a solitary desk chair and a bare double mattress. Beside the mattress was a pile of trash, topped with a half-eaten hamburger. It looked as if someone else had stayed there after Sabrina and her granddaughter's departure.

Robert snapped photos and left.

• • •

After looking around, Jocelyn and I went to the kitchen.

"Please stay for a cup of tea, Jocelyn."

I didn't want to be alone—not yet.

Our kettle was on the stove. I filled it and put the burner on. The fridge was empty, but I found some herbal tea.

"I can't stay long."

"I'm going to clean up the place this afternoon and go through our things to make sure everything's okay."

Suddenly the front door opened, then came footsteps. Before I knew it, Sabrina and another woman—also a realtor, I learned—were with us in the kitchen.

"Get out, Allison," Sabrina screamed at me. "You have no right to be here. I'll have you both arrested for trespassing."

Astounded, I hesitated, then tried to reason with her.

"Sabrina, you know perfectly well I have a right to be here. Why haven't you been paying rent? It looks like you moved out, but you still owe us back rent."

"Get out, get out, if you don't leave there'll be *violence*."

Was she going to hit me? Her screeching didn't stop. I glanced at Jocelyn, who looked shocked.

Sabrina picked up the phone and dialed the police.

"Let's wait in the library until she calms down," I murmured to Jocelyn.

Sabrina was ranting into the phone.

In the library, I asked Jocelyn if she would fetch my handbag from the car. As I waited at the door leading to the garage, I felt it slam against me, pushing me into the garage. Sabrina had locked the door, so I went around to the front door and walked inside. Seeing that she was back in the kitchen on the phone, I shut the library door and sat on the couch, lacing my fingers together to keep them from trembling. Yet my hands kept moving as if they had a life of their own.

Jocelyn returned with my bag and sat in a nearby chair. We talked quietly, haltingly.

The alarm company representative arrived, as pre-arranged, to reset the alarm code, but he was interrupted by Sabrina bursting into the library, shrieking. It was impossible to talk, so he gave me an emergency code and left.

The doorbell rang.

I opened the door to find a state trooper with a squat, stocky build and a dour expression. I invited him in.

"Hello. I'm Allison Drew, and this is my father's house. The tenant's in the kitchen." I gestured the way.

The trooper planted his legs wide apart and leaned forward.

"I know you. I spoke to you on the phone. I'm telling you now, this is *not* going to end well for you."

Shocked, I said nothing but watched him go to the kitchen to speak to Sabrina.

Only several months later would I learn that this was Trooper Calvin Lowman.

I went back to the library and shut the door.

Jocelyn rose to go.

As she did so, a slim, twenty-something trooper entered from the garage and introduced himself as Trooper Flannigan. He had an eager air with attractive, even features.

I explained the situation, showing him my lease and pointing out the clause that stated: *"Landlords have the right to visit and to occupy one of the spare bedrooms, and they will give tenants reasonable notice of their intent to visit."*

"That's a very unusual clause."

Really?

Perhaps it was unusual, but Americans have many types of house-sharing agreements. Still stung by Trooper Lowman's words, I didn't reply, but sat down again on the couch.

Trooper Lowman appeared in the library, mentioning a letter from the tenant's lawyer. I didn't understand.

"Here's my lease and an email from my lawyer," I replied, reaching up with the documents. "The lease gives me and my sister the right to stay at the house."

He waved dismissively.

"I'm not interested in your papers. This is what's going to happen. You are going to be arrested. You will be taken to Troop B. Stand up and turn around."

I sat there, my brain whirring.

Arrested?

How could he know who was legally in the house without reading the lease? Hadn't he received any training about the need to examine the lease? The *Landlord/Tenant Disputes Police Training Manual* gave four reasons leading to possible arrest, but none of them applied to my situation.

I was stunned. But I stood up.

"Do you mind if I use the bathroom?" I said, pointing to the right. "It's just there, in the hall."

He blocked my path.

"I'd like to call my attorney." He mentioned the scarf draped around my neck.

"Oh, my scarf. It's too warm to tie it."

He took a step forward—sixteen inches away—and, leaning towards me, barked in my face:

"Take the scarf off and put it in your bag." I felt instantly, viscerally, like a small animal confronted by a larger one, that Trooper Lowman would not hesitate to hit me.

I removed the scarf.

"Turn around."

I turned.

"Do you have any weapons?"

"No ... I don't believe in guns."

He frisked me, running his hands down my hips and legs.

"Put your hands behind your back."

I did.

He handcuffed me.

The very moment that I felt the heavy metal cuffs around my wrists—even before they were locked—my relationship with the world changed utterly. A surge of intense panic swept through my head and my chest as I *experienced* what it is to be physically deprived of one's freedom. Captive. Prisoner. What would I do if I had to experience this sensation for days, weeks, months, years even?

Would I lose my mind?

Surely I would.

An image of a slave flashed across my mind.

I now knew something that no book can ever teach, no amount of empathy can ever approximate.

And how I wish I had never learned it. How I wish I still knew about handcuffs only from films and TV. How I wish I still had the luxury of empathy.

Seconds ticked by.

Somehow, I found my tongue.

"How many times have you been called to domestic disputes where a husband was beating a wife, but left without making an arrest? And now you arrest me for *sitting in my home*?"

Trooper Flannigan moved behind me, grabbed my shoulders and propelled me forward into the garage, out of the house and to the police car.

It was hard not to fall, trying to balance with my hands locked behind me and someone pushing me.

Jocelyn was still there; her car had been blocked by the police vehicles.

"Lo ... look what they've done Jocelyn." My voice cracked. "They've arrested me for sitting in my home." She approached but the trooper waved her away. He strapped me in the car, got in and proudly brandished a paper.

"I'm going to read you your Miranda rights."

"I want to call my attorney."

"You can make all the calls you want at the station."

He fastened his seatbelt and began driving.

As I sat there handcuffed, he prattled gaily, "My brother's in London. He's doing a legal internship there." He had watched silently while the other trooper arrested me, instead of telling his colleague that he had seen my lease and read the clause giving me the right to be in the house. His chatter was unbearable. My mind heaved.

• • •

My previous visits to Troop B barracks had been to enquire about progress on Daddy's case. On those occasions, I had walked up the front steps to the main entrance. This time Trooper Flannigan parked in the rear. He pulled me out of the car, then pushed me from behind, steering me down steep concrete stairs—I almost tumbled—and through a door into a small basement room, sparsely furnished with a few cabinets, a desk in one corner and a chair on either side.

Trooper Flannigan took out a key and removed the handcuffs.

"*Now*, you can use the restroom." He gestured with his head. "The door must stay open."

The restroom door was clear glass.

I looked at him in disbelief.

"But you can see me."

"I'll turn around."

"But you can still hear me."

I had to go. I thought they were going to put me in a cell, and from what I had seen on TV, I would have even less privacy.

Why didn't they have a woman on duty, I wondered, so that women prisoners were not compelled to use the toilet in front of men?

Trooper Flannigan told me to sit at the desk facing him while he read the charges – criminal trespass and criminal breach of peace; the place – my home. I gasped. I would later learn that the maximum penalty for these charges, if I were found guilty, would be one and one-half years of prison, a $3,000 fine and five years' probation.

He fingerprinted and photographed me.

Humiliated, I worried how I would look in a mug shot.

"Allison!"

It was Lieutenant Leonard. The very same man who for two years I had begged to speed up the investigation into Daddy's vanishing, and about whom I had complained to the police commissioner and the state's attorney just the week before.

"I don't understand why I've been arrested. I have a valid lease."

"You've been arrested on the authorization of the state's attorney. Have your attorney call the state's attorney."

He and Trooper Flannigan now began counting the money in my handbag. Trooper Lowman passed swiftly, silently through the room on his way outside, a queasy smile on his face. I turned to Lieutenant Leonard.

"If this arrest is illegal," I looked him in the eyes, "I will sue the Connecticut State Police."

"Okay. If you go back to your house, you will be rearrested."

"What about my father's case?"

Finished counting, he rose, turned on his heels and left the room.

Trooper Flannigan handed me some forms to sign and informed me of my court date. Then he pointed to the back door.

"Now, you can leave and call your lawyer."

Disoriented, I climbed the concrete stairs. The building, the parked cars seemed slightly askew as if the ground had subtly shifted. Trooper Flannigan followed to drive me to my car, which was at the house.

Daddy's house was my only American domicile. I had no place to go—but was obliged to remain for the January court date. My clothes, legal documents and mail were at the house, but the police wouldn't allow me access to get them—despite my legal right to do so.

I drove to Jocelyn's; she couldn't put me up.

I called Ilene, a member of Daddy's church, and burst into tears. She took me in. I borrowed a robe and slippers. I was wearing boots, but had to buy shoes. Throughout the holidays, Daddy's house remained dark and uninhabited, so my realtor Robert told me.

CHAPTER 16

"Why would Sabrina still claim tenancy if she's no longer living at the house?" I asked Ilene and her husband as we sat at their kitchen table that evening.

I had been resting in their spare bedroom, jotting down notes about the day. I didn't have a smart phone to tape the day's events. But recording the evidence presented by my eyes and ears, putting my observations, thoughts and feelings on paper gave me some sense of agency, even if I felt raw and powerless, caught up in events over which I had little or no control. Now I needed to talk.

"Maybe she needs the address so her granddaughter can go to school here," Ilene speculated.

"That makes sense. But where's the girl living? Her mother's in Hartford. If she wants her daughter to go to school here, why doesn't she move here?" We couldn't figure it out.

Nor did I understand why I had been arrested.

"What did you do?" my lawyer asked when I called him.

"I didn't do anything! I was sitting on my couch. The cop never asked me to leave."

The morning after the arrest Daddy's friend Brooke phoned me. She had been away when he disappeared but wrote to me after her return. I called her, and she was sympathetic, inviting me to her house several times. She told me she had been unnerved by her few encounters with Pamela, but she spoke warmly of Sabrina. The three of us went for a drink one evening after listening to Michael Dooling talk about his missing persons book. An engaging speaker, he sparked a lively discussion. A man in the audience asked about Daddy's case, and I spoke up, expressing disappointment that the police still hadn't secured the needed phone and internet records, nor even interviewed the first witness.

This morning Brooke sounded gleeful.

"I just spoke to my friend. She confirmed Sabrina befriended her, but then called the police on her, just like she did with you."

"Why didn't you tell me this before, Brooke?" I had thought ... hoped she was my friend.

"I knew my friend had a problem with Sabrina, but I didn't know what it was ... I don't like to gossip."

"What happened to your friend?"

"The police went to her house, spoke to her and left laughing." She chuckled.

"Brooke, what's your friend's name? I need to understand why the police arrested me when they didn't arrest her. I'd really like to talk to her."

"Oh, I can't give you her name."

"Why not?"

"My friend doesn't want to get involved." I pleaded, but she hung up. I never heard another word from her.

• • •

I stepped through the looking glass into a parallel world known as the criminal justice system, where lawyers make a quick and easy buck from "plea bargains" and Kafkaesque "accelerated rehabilitation" programs. My civil lawyer transferred me to his colleague, a criminal lawyer. Neither mentioned that their work relationship posed a conflict of interest in case I chose to go to trial.

A garrulous sixty-something character planning a vacation to England with his wife, the criminal lawyer assured me—before I wrote the check—that he expected to get the charges dropped.

He was seeing the state's attorney at a party that very evening.

And he made no bones that "the police lie."

Connecticut's police had just been hit by scandal; the case made the *New York Times*. The Justice Department found that the East Haven Police Department was terrorizing the Latino community with biased policing, unconstitutional search and seizure and excessive force. Father Jim Manship of St. Rose of Lima Church had offered to help by filming examples of police intimidation. For his troubles he had been arrested; the arresting officer had reworked his report twenty-seven times in an attempt to justify the arrest. The charges against Father Manship were eventually dismissed, and in January 2012 the FBI arrested a sergeant and three officers on charges of conspiracy, false arrest, excessive force and obstruction of justice. Two pleaded guilty; two were found guilty after trial; all were sentenced to prison.

My first experience of criminal court—at the Bantam courthouse, a low, flat building fronted by a parking lot, a ten-minute, down-market drive from the Litchfield County courthouse. I was there with my new friend Alice, a charming, stylish nonagenarian who kindly put me up after I left Ilene's.

"Are you a lawyer?" an armed guard, a woman, asked me as I put my handbag through the scanner.

"No, I'm an alleged criminal."

Silently, she handed me my bag.

The courthouse was noisy with the din of countless conversations, its overheated halls smelling faintly of sweat. The benches along the corridors were full, people without a seat roaming the halls.

Aside from myself and a well-dressed man on a drunk-driving charge, the plaintiffs, all white, were working class and clearly disadvantaged. This showed in their K-Mart clothes, their lackluster skin and the fatigue and stress etched across their pale faces. A thin woman in a faded pink track suit, the fabric shiny at the knees, leaned against a wall staring vacantly, flicking back the shoulder-length dark blond hair falling into her eyes.

Those who could afford lawyers were seated across from the courtroom door; those who couldn't sat around the corner and down the hall. Waiting nervously directly opposite the courtroom, I took a pen and notepad from my handbag and began taking notes.

A trim well-dressed woman sporting a short, no-nonsense hair cut came up and introduced herself as a reporter. To my surprise, she confessed that she, too, had been a victim of what I thought was white-collar rent fraud. Unlike other Connecticut judicial districts, at the time Litchfield County didn't put housing court information online, so home owners and landlords couldn't check out prospective tenants. This made northwest Connecticut prime territory for rent fraud.

The reporter had rented to a professional couple, who, like Sabrina, had stopped paying rent after a few months. Like Sabrina, they then claimed the house was uninhabitable. It had taken the woman almost a year to evict the couple. She knew of similar cases.

"Why don't you write an article about this? Do an exposé? It would be a public service," I said.

"I would if I could, but I can't get enough people to come forward."

"I'll come forward. Until you expose this, it'll continue."

A few days later a Canaan lawyer would tell me about his client, whose tenants, also professionals, had stopped paying rent a few months after moving in, claiming the house was uninhabitable and refusing the landlord access to check.

"Why would they want to stay in an uninhabitable house?" he pondered aloud.

It seemed I wasn't alone.

After some time, my lawyer told me to enter the courtroom, a square, high-ceilinged room with wooden benches, and the judge's platform at the front. Alice and I sat on a bench to the left; my lawyer chattered while we waited for the session to begin. He told us he believed everyone was guilty, even Peter Reilly. He had gone through the Reilly police file and was convinced they'd got the right man, despite his exoneration. Alice later confided she had been appalled by the lawyer's attitude, but I was too distracted with worry to consider the implications of his words.

My lawyer told me to move to the other side.

A door opened at the front left corner of the courtroom. Five young men shuffled in, Anglos or perhaps Latinos, shackled together at their ankles, accompanied by an armed guard. It was the first time I had seen men in chains in person. I had thought they only used chains in the South.

But here they were in wealthy, sophisticated Litchfield County with its Manhattanites and Hollywood stars.

A door at the front right opened.

Enter the judge, a thin, grey-haired, slightly-stooped man who sat down and began droning tonelessly, staring into the distance. I heard the judge say, "Miranda rights," then abruptly stop talking. The chained men were led away. Only then did I realize that the judge had been addressing them, without once looking at them.

It was my turn.

My case was called only to be continued—postponed—at the request of housing prosecutor, Judith R. Dicine, who was not present.

Later, I texted Jack about the chains.

"I thought they only did that in the South," he replied.

He must have read my mind.

• • •

A small victory—I won in Housing Court, which operates under civil law. Sabrina hadn't paid rent in four months. She used her granddaughter as leverage and was given one month's grace as long as she paid the equivalent of the monthly rent—which she did, in the nick of time—with a deadline of February 29, 2012 to vacate completely. I was allowed to go to my home, make photographs and gather my personal effects. The house was still unlived in, the heating still at 50. Sabrina had left signs on the furniture with large printed messages:

Dirty, mouse-infested sofa; *Stained, smelly chair*, *Broken lamp*.

• • •

I returned to York and collapsed in exhaustion. My doctor signed me off work for a month. I felt as if I had been through a meat grinder, and it was so wonderful to do nothing but rest. Margo was ecstatic, convinced she now had a round-the-clock playmate.

Back at work, I met with my graduate student Eudora Kombo, a Nigerian-born American and a retired professor, who'd decided to write a Master's thesis on women and armed struggle in African liberation movements.

At our first meeting, I sat behind my desk, and she sat on the other side, observing me. We discussed her research plan. Then, in a soft, melodious voice, her dangling earrings shimmering as she shifted her head, she began telling me about her losses. Because she opened herself to me, I found myself confiding in her about Daddy's disappearance and my arrest. We became friends, visited each other's homes and spent several wonderful afternoons at the Yorkshire Sculpture Park.

Those familiar with the American criminal justice system know about the cozy relationship between police and prosecutors. *Perry Mason*'s nemesis Prosecutor Hamilton Burger once avowed being more committed to finding the truth than to winning his case; his admission inspired future Supreme Court Justice Sonia Sotomayor to become a prosecutor. But even if that TV show had once approximated real life, it's no longer the case.

Hopeful after the Housing Court decision, I was very distressed when my criminal lawyer informed me the housing prosecutor wouldn't be dropping the charges. Fiftyish, with a ponytail and a too-tight, too-short skirt when I eventually saw her—was she the state's attorney to whom Lieutenant Leonard had referred, or was it David Shepack—or had the lieutenant been bluffing?

The housing prosecutor, a practitioner in residence at the University of New Haven, was, I discovered via the university web site, an Adjunct Certified Police Instructor for the Connecticut Police Officer Standard and Training Council. The guidelines Trooper Lowman had seemingly breached, had been prepared by the very prosecutor who was now coming after me:

"The only occupants who may be arrested for trespassing are 'true' trespassers, i.e., persons who moved into the unit without the consent of either the landlord or the tenant."

Sabrina's signed consent was on the lease, which she had written.

The day of the housing court deadline Sabrina dropped by Daddy's neighbor Otto's to say she had moved out. But that afternoon Otto told me her car was still in the driveway.

Sabrina also called my realtor Robert and told him she had left. But she hadn't returned the key or the garage door opener. The phone and electricity were still in her name; the heating fuel was billed to her real estate firm.

My civil lawyer secured a court order for a Marshall to ensure she left.

Robert, in the meantime, had decided that his professional relationship with Sabrina was more important than his position as my realtor. When the Marshall called him for the house key, he told him not to come. The Marshall showed up, nonetheless, but Sabrina was in the process of removing her few items, which he allowed her to do.

I had left a spare house key with Otto in case of emergencies and now asked him to let my handyman use it to check the house.

"After your arrest I called the police and asked what to do with the spare key. The trooper told me to turn it over to the tenant, so I did," he said.

"Why didn't you contact me? I could have collected the key while I was there if you no longer wanted it."

"I did what the trooper said."

"But why did you call the police? It wasn't a police matter."

"Well, you'd been arrested."

"That's irrelevant. That was my key. The trooper had no right to tell you what to do with it."

I realized now that my arrest had stigmatized me—no matter that four lawyers had confirmed that the lease was decisive, that I was legally in my father's house and that the arrest, accordingly, was illegal. Despite the *Lakeville Journal*'s taciturn approach to Daddy's case, I had made its "police blotter." As with Daddy's disappearance, most people in Salisbury responded to my situation with silence.

Doing research, I learned that the presumption of innocence—incorporated into the thirteenth-century Magna Carta to protect individuals from arbitrary imprisonment—has been seriously eroded in American law.

The presumption of innocence is rooted in two due process clauses in our Bill of Rights. The Fifth Amendment states that no person shall "be deprived of life, liberty, or property, without due process of law." The

Fourteenth Amendment, enacted after the Civil War to ensure the rights of former slaves, adds "nor shall any State deprive any person of life, liberty, or property, without due process of law."

The legal interpretation of due process shifted significantly from the 1960s to the 1980s, when the presumption of innocence and the acceptance of pretrial liberty for all but capital crimes were overshadowed by a clamor for public safety with strong racial overtones. This change went hand in hand with an increasing public trust in the police—at least amongst white middle-class Americans.

Judges assumed more powers to determine pretrial guilt. Pretrial detention came to be seen, not as punishment, but as a legitimate means to promote public order. The presumption of innocence shifted from the assumption of *pretrial innocence* to the narrow notion of the prosecutor's burden during trial to prove guilt beyond a reasonable doubt. Today, from the moment of arrest to the preliminary hearings to the plea bargains, you are *presumed guilty*. The presumption of innocence operates *only* during trial.

If the judge orders pretrial detention, your fate is effectively sealed. When you are detained before trial, you have less negotiating power. Few people can afford bail, and pretrial detention generally leads to a custodial sentence after trial. If you go to trial, you have the right to argue your innocence, but the burden is actually on you. Since most people who are arrested don't have the resources to prove their innocence they take plea bargains. Nowadays, I discovered, very few cases go to trial—about two percent at the federal level, for example—so even the narrow presumption of innocence at trial no longer applies for most arrested people.

I remembered Bettina's friend Edwin, a willowy young white man and a poet who'd had a troubled childhood. One summer he had stayed at Daddy's house—a "house of books," he called it. In the mornings he and Bettina wrote and read each other's work. In the afternoons he perused our bookshelves and read voraciously. Once, after gazing at Maufra's *Sacré-Coeur*, he picked up a book on Impressionist painting and read about the artist.

Edwin liked working outside. Chopping wood one day, he spied a bear, twenty feet away, staring at him.

"Hello bear," he murmured. Eyes downcast, he backed slowly away, as did the bear—intuitively, Edwin did just what outdoor experts advise.

Years before, as a teenager, Edwin had been arrested for using drugs.

"They told me if I didn't take the six-month plea they'd throw the book at me and give me the longest sentence they could—ten years. I couldn't take the chance."

The prison was divided between Black Muslims and White Aryans—no safe place for loners—so he converted to Islam and joined the Black Muslims. In for a felony, he lost his right to vote before he had a chance to use it.

Otto had known me for thirty years and professed indignation with Sabrina's failure to pay rent. Once I was arrested, though, he wanted no further contact—even for a key. Not only has the presumption of innocence been eroded in law. The presumption of guilt has permeated American culture. America's endless police shows portray the cops as honest, hard-working and intelligent, while depicting those they arrest as deserving of it. The alleged wrong-doers are generally blacks or poor whites derided as trash. Aggregated Gallup polls for 2015-2017 indicate that 61 per cent of whites, 45 per cent of Hispanics and only 30 percent of blacks have a great deal or quite a lot of confidence in the police. For many Americans—especially whites—convincing themselves that other people get arrested because they deserve it allows them to feel safe from arbitrary arrest.

I, too, had had my preconceptions. Despite my eventual, painful realization that Troop B personnel were uninterested in solving Daddy's case, I had sought to convince myself that this was due to the Northwest corner's peculiar small-town politics. On TV and at the movies I had often heard the proverbial claim, "the cops are lying." Yet I had still clung to my belief in the overall honesty of the police. Solving Daddy's case, finding him so that he could be buried, depended on that belief. I had read about miscarriages of justice and police brutality and racism in the cities, but I had nonetheless assumed that they were exceptions happening far from me. Had I been blinded by the white middle-class privilege that people speak about? Absolutely.

• • •

I received the arrest report in March. I read it, I reread it slowly, and then I read it again. One thought filled my mind, swelling my brain till I felt it would explode.

The Connecticut State Police are capable of anything.

The implications of the four-page report were overwhelming. This account of my arrest and the events in the house and at Troop B differed markedly from mine. Despite the grammatical errors, the report seemed slick, as if the trooper had written many such documents to justify arrests.

"Tfc. [Boyd] stayed on the phone with [Sabrina] ... and he asked [her] to instruct DREW, who refused to speak to Tfc [Boyd], to leave the residence and wait in her vehicle until the police arrived. DREW refused."

Virtually every statement of the arrest report had errors of fact, in my view. But they were skillfully presented to suggest I had come to the house with the intention of getting arrested.

"DREW refused to leave the residence and wait in her car when given instructions from, [sic] who she believed was a police officer on the telephone, and in fact was TFC. [Boyd]. DREW stated to me that she was not going to leave the residence unless she was under arrest."

Surprisingly, the trooper didn't claim he had asked me to leave—he hadn't. And he twice acknowledged witnessing me take my lease from my handbag and refer to it. But he didn't state he read the lease—he hadn't.

Later, under the Freedom of Information Act, I would access the recording of Sabrina's call from the house while she was in the kitchen.

"She lives in York, England," Sabrina tells Trooper Boyd. "She has no business being here. She's been threatening to do this. We're going through a legal proceeding."

The trooper confers with some other troopers.

"There is a confrontation between the landlord and tenant. Allison Drew is actually on the premises right now."

"You might want to ask her to leave the property until she has completed the eviction process."

"Mrs Drew is there with another lady?" the trooper asks Sabrina.

"Yes."

"Not making any judgment, would it be easier for you to remove yourself?"

"No I'm not leaving the house. They need to get out of here."

"Can you put Allison on the phone? Can I speak to Allison?"

"I'd prefer that you'd come here."

"The troopers are out ... If you do not want to leave, put Allison on the phone, and I'll tell her to leave."

Silence.

"You need to step outside," Sabrina states. "The officers are coming."

A long pause.

Jocelyn and I weren't in the kitchen. How could I respond when I couldn't hear her?

"Are they coming now?" Sabrina asks the trooper. "She refuses to step outside."

"Mrs Drew refuses to leave," the trooper tells his colleague, who begins talking to a third person.

"Mrs Drew is refusing to leave the residence."

"Allison is there now."

"Drew needs to respect a court order. She should not be at the residence. We have a letter from an attorney stating that Drew should not be in the building, on the premises."

"How did she get in? Does she have a key?" Trooper Boyd asks Sabrina.

"She has a key. My attorney told me to change the locks ... and I decided not to. I should have." Another long pause.

"What is Mrs Drew doing?"

"Yes?"

"What are they doing right now?"

"She's sitting here in the kitchen. You need to get her out."

Jocelyn and I were in the library with the door shut. Sabrina's lawyer didn't tell her to change the locks. There was no court order. The police accepted her claims at face value, not bothering to check any of them.

She played them like a fiddle.

CHAPTER 17

By now I had become expert at checking the claims made by the police against the documents I received through the different sources at my disposal. Insistently following one line of enquiry only, the detectives investigating Daddy's disappearance had sometimes equivocated, so it seemed, when we discussed the case. The arrest report, however, was in a different league. The word of the police officer is the foundation of the entire criminal justice edifice. Shouldn't prosecutors and judges, with all their expensive law degrees, be able to spot implausible claims, inconsistencies, lies?

Apparently not.

In mid-March I spoke at an international conference on "Algerian and Arab Revolutions" at the University of Portsmouth. Just before dinner my criminal lawyer texted and asked me to call.

"We're going to push for Accelerated Rehabilitation," he told me.

"Why?" I asked, baffled.

To push for this meant the suspension of the right to trial. According to the Sixth Amendment to the Bill of Rights: "In all criminal prosecutions, the accused shall enjoy the right to a speedy and public trial by an impartial jury of the state and district wherein the crime shall have been committed."

It was very distressing that any legal procedure would suspend one of our crucial constitutional rights. I couldn't make heads or tails of his explanation of the program.

"Why can't I go to trial?"

"You have the *right* to trial, but it isn't worth the risk. Whatever the merits of your case, juries are unpredictable."

I was dismayed.

After the call I joined my colleagues, most of them Muslim, drinking little if any alcohol. I slurped down two glasses of wine and raised my empty glass to signal the waitress—*another glass, please,* to blot out the fear. My colleagues watched silently, their eyebrows raised.

Then began the continuances.

Twelve in all, most of them courtesy of the prosecutor. No right to a speedy anything, so it seemed, as far as she was concerned. Tormented by insomnia, my worries whirred endlessly around my head. Would my case go on forever, like Daddy's?

"It's disgusting," said a State of Connecticut employee familiar with the criminal justice system. "They drop charges all the time. Just the other day they dropped the charges on a murder case."

"Then why won't the prosecutor drop mine since I had the legal right to be in my home?"

"I don't know," came the reply.

I sent out queries on academic discussion lists about illegal arrests, hoping to find people with similar experiences, but getting precious little back.

More research. Daily life has become criminalized, I learned, as courts give the police arbitrary power to stop, detain and arrest—even for activities such as eating in public places, which would not have been considered a crime in the past.

Take the French fry case—Hedgepeth vs. Washington Metro Authority. The case was widely reported, from the *Washington Post* to the *Los Angeles Times*. In October 2000 a twelve-year-old girl bought a bag of French fries on her way home from school. Waiting for her friend to buy a Metro ticket, but before going through the fare-gate, she ate a fry. Minors were prohibited from eating in the Metro. A transit policer officer hovering nearby waited for her to go through the gate then arrested her for eating. So what if she cried?

At the station, she was fingerprinted, booked, and, her shoelaces removed, detained for several hours at a juvenile processing center. Her lawyer argued that the law against eating on the Metro unfairly targeted minors. But five years later Judge John G. Roberts—future Chief Justice of the United States—upheld the arrest's constitutionality.

There are many such cases in which commonplace activities, sometimes annoying, are deemed illegal. Waiting at the Harlem-125th Street Metro North train station, a man approached me.

"Can you give me five dollars?"

Reaching into my bag, I took out a handful of coins.

"Can I keep all that?"

"Sure." He moved down the platform. Less than a minute later I heard metal clanking noisily on the ground. Two cops were pushing the man against a wall, handcuffing him.

"We got him," one of them yelled, as two others arrived.

"I don't want that money," the man said, his eyes staring darkly through me at his imagined future.

"You don't want the money?" one cop asked, while the others laughed. Four white cops for one black beggar. Although the constitution's First Amendment protects the right to beg, New York City transit prohibits it. If you're hungry, asking for money will get you arrested. And the crucial right to free movement in public space, which courts used to uphold against police interference, has virtually vanished in the name of security.

The courts claim the police must be able to use their judgment on the spot. But the judgment of the modestly-educated, inadequately-trained police is notoriously poor. Hence, they rely on stereotypes. They are racially biased. They over-arrest and brutalize people. There are far too many unnecessary arrests for the congested courts to handle. Thus, the widespread use of easy money-making rackets like plea bargains and accelerated rehabilitation programs.

Looking back, I felt I wasn't well served by either of my lawyers—and not only because they failed to declare the potential conflict of interest stemming from their work relationship.

My civil lawyer insisted he had warned me when I phoned him that I would "likely" be arrested if I went to Daddy's house. Well, I didn't hear that. Why hadn't he put his alleged warning in writing after our conversation? Even more amazingly, he claimed I said I was "prepared in the event." That was a brazen lie. I had hired him to ensure that I was following the law and thus wouldn't be arrested. I felt sick when I read his letter.

Nor did the criminal lawyer explain my possible options at the outset; I had to drag the information from him bit by bit. And he was seemingly too weak to confront the judge and prosecutor about the endless continuances.

"We met with the judge who indicated that he thought the matter should be disposed of either by Accelerated Rehabilitation, with a relatively short period of time or a simple trespass, creating a public disturbance, which are not criminal charges but are infractions," he informed me.

He began pushing this second option.

But in that case, he acknowledged, the prosecutor would insist the criminal charges remain on my record for eighteen months. Only then would they be removed. Having these criminal charges dangling over me for this additional period would put me at further risk of what I saw as police retaliation if I complained about their inadequate handling of Daddy's case.

Why should I have to bear those charges when I was legally in my home? Why would the prosecutor want to criminalize me?

Six months after my arrest my lawyer replied to these questions.

"The main complaint the prosecutor has is that they feel when you were asked to leave and you didn't, you gave the cops a hard time. I know you hotly contest those facts but that is what we are dealing with here."

So, according to his account, the prosecutor was evidently more concerned with upholding the police claims than with upholding the law. Not the world of Hamilton Burger.

Still worried about police retaliation, I contacted the Office of the Victim Advocate, which gave me much useful advice on missing persons cases. I also contacted Congressman Murphy again, requesting help transferring Daddy's case from Troop B and getting my DNA removed from police records and suggesting the need for a civilian oversight committee to assess cases of alleged police retaliation. Once again I heard from his aide, who informed me the police said they would contact me directly. I was never able to get my DNA removed, despite my repeated appeals.

• • •

Back at my first court appearance in January I had been struck by the sight of young men in ankle chains. Now, summertime, I saw women in ankle chains. It was warm. The women, all white, mostly young, were in skirts, bare-legged. Why were they chained? A woman of indeterminate age, thin, with long greying hair, complained loudly.

"Oh my god, they're killing me. I have cuts all around my ankles. Why can't you take them off? I promise I won't run away."

How could she run away? The courtroom was always full of armed guards. Peter Reilly had also complained about the chains, wrote Donald Connery. Transported to prison, he recalled "hobbling out of the car with those chains on. They were hurting my legs."

The woman wailed.

No one in authority batted an eye.

I took notes.

I didn't have the stamina, the money or the time to fly to the United States every few months to deal with this matter.

I switched lawyers.

My new lawyer, tall, slim and striking, came to the house to see the scene of the arrest; she understood the issues. We discussed whether I should go for a jury trial or trial by judge. She advised against trial by judge. The links between the judges and the police were just too strong. They ate at the same restaurants and slapped each other on the back each time they put someone away.

We began preparing for a jury trial.

Sabrina listed her home address as a Vermont post office box—someone forwarded her mail—and I realized she had been driving around with Vermont license plates for years, even though Connecticut stipulates that out-of-state plates must be changed within two months. It turned out she was listed as president of a Hartford organization whose board of directors included two dead people. I then learned she had switched her phone number to a Lakeville house belonging to a dead woman—one of the Town of Salisbury's few African-American homeowners—whose house had not yet gone through probate. I drove by the house and saw Sabrina's possessions on the porches.

Robert, the realtor I had used after Sabrina, was a member of the Litchfield County Board of Realtors. He had previously offered his opinion that Sabrina's actions violated their ethical code. I spoke at length with a representative from the Litchfield County Board of Realtors, who emphatically assured me they took ethical violations extremely seriously. She sent me some complex forms for filing an ethics complaint. When I phoned back, she said that my complaint concerned Sabrina as a *tenant*, but they only dealt with complaints against individuals in their capacity as *realtors*. I duly dropped this line of action.

I would later learn that, in her efforts to deny me access to Daddy's house, Sabrina had used the same Falls Village lawyer who'd represented Pamela. Ironically, he ended up taking Sabrina to court twice for non-payment of legal fees. I found that she had a list of small claims cases against her. And when I eventually went to the Salisbury library to check Sabrina's listing of our house, I saw that she had priced it similarly to those with swimming pools or lakefront access that were conveniently close to the train station. It seemed to me that she had overpriced our home precisely so that it wouldn't rent.

My new lawyer was confident we could get the charges dropped or win the case, should the State pursue it, which she doubted. But I couldn't face another year in the criminal justice system. Another year of sleeplessness, of feeling trapped in a morass of institutionalized indifference and moral corruption.

At the last minute I panicked and told my lawyer I would take Accelerated Rehabilitation.

At the next court date, I signed the form—three weeks probation, no conditions.

But when I started writing the check, I couldn't make myself sign it. I had changed my mind.

I wanted to go to trial.

My lawyer submitted the paperwork.

I went to court.

Judge Upton was presiding.

You've already had your chance to speak, he said, as I began introducing myself.

I felt squashed, intimidated.

Both white and middle class, he and I might have met at a party where I might have told him about my Algerian research, about *le pouvoir*, and asked him about life as a Connecticut judge. But here I was, presumed guilty, stigmatized as a criminal, just as Daddy had been stigmatized as a dementia sufferer—not worth bothering with.

My lawyer stated I wanted to go to trial.

The prosecutor began stammering.

The judge replied he would read a motion.

My lawyer submitted the motion.

The judge denied it. No explanation.

My lawyer submitted another motion.

Once again, the judge denied it. No explanation. He waived the fee, considered the accelerated rehabilitation a done deal. Of course, I could have appealed it all the way up. I was angry. I wanted to fight for my right to trial. But I wasn't emotionally strong enough. And I didn't have the money. And besides, what proportion of judicial decisions were overturned when you had the French fry case to consider?

So I ate my anger, swallowing it whole.

Denied my right to trial, I looked up the Judicial District Movement of Criminal Cases on the State of Connecticut Judicial Branch web site. During 2012-13, 7 out of 285 Litchfield County cases or 2.46 percent were disposed by trial. Statewide that year, 188 out of 2994 cases or 6.28 percent were disposed by trial. During 2013-14, the numbers were respectively 2.46 and 5.6 percent. By 2016-17, the numbers had declined to 0.5 and 5.1 percent. In 2017-18, 2 out of 215 Litchfield County criminal cases or 0.9 percent were disposed of by trial. Statewide, the figures that year were 121 out of 2,377 cases or 5.1 percent.

As at the federal level, Connecticut's right to trial has slipped by the wayside unnoticed. Plea bargains are imposed on the innocent by police seeking credit for arrests, only too willing to lie, backed up by prosecutors eager to prove the police right and by lawyers seeking a fast buck.

Other state statistics are similar or even worse. The criminal trial remains at the center of countless TV shows, movies and thrillers. Yet our right to trial has been dangerously eroded, replaced by a soulless bureaucracy that has mushroomed in response to over-arresting, facilitated by those judges and prosecutors who condone police abuse of power. The entire system rests on the cult of the policeman who does no wrong. Is it truly a surprise that the United States has 2.2 million people in jail and prison—more than any other country—and more prisoners per 100,000 inhabitants? Fifty percent of American adults have had an immediate family member incarcerated for at least one night, and sixty-four percent have had an immediate or extended family member in jail or prison, according to the 2018 Cornell University-Fwd.us study, *Every Second: The impact of the incarceration crisis on American families*.

Yet we still sing in our national anthem of "the land of the free."

Is it too late to win back our right to trial?

Our Second Amendment, unlike the sixth, is often in the news: "A well-regulated militia being necessary to the security of a free state, the right of the people to keep and bear arms shall not be infringed."

How is it possible that so many Americans fight for the right to bear arms, but so few for the right to trial?

• • •

I read up on the Billy Smolinski case. When Smolinski vanished in 2004, the Waterbury police responded sluggishly. Critical of their lethargic approach, Billy's family put up flyers across western Connecticut, only to find them torn down. Then Billy's mom Jan was arrested by the Woodbridge Police for posting a flyer and charged with trespassing and disorderly conduct—the state's attorney later dropped the charges. Learning about Jan's arrest—although several years after the fact—was enough to intimidate me from posting more flyers, especially after my own arrest. I also discovered that Billy's ex-girlfriend had sued Jan and her daughter for defamation. With the ex-girlfriend's claims supported by the local police whom Jan Smolinski had criticized, in 2012 a state superior court ordered that the Smolinskis pay her compensation. I felt the Connecticut police were waging war against families of missing persons who complained about police incompetence.

Closer to home, I heard about Mark Lauretano, a retired state trooper who was one of Salisbury's three selectmen—officials serving as the chief administrative authority in New England towns. Based at Troop B, he had been Salisbury's resident trooper. In 1999 he had taken the state police to court, and in 2006 he had won a $450,000 settlement affirming state troopers' rights to free speech. Donald Connery, known locally for his Peter Reilly book, wrote about the case in the *Litchfield County Times* and the *Lakeville Journal*.

The dispute originated with a case involving the Hotchkiss School.

A fourteen-year-old African-American boy from Brooklyn, New York, recipient of a prestigious four-year Oliver Scholarship, claimed that during the night of February 28, 1997 two white boys had entered his room and that one pinned him down while the other sodomized him. His room was dark, but he recognized them from their silhouettes and voices; they were in his classes and had previously racially harassed him. However, he couldn't identify who held him down and who raped him. That term his emotional state deteriorated rapidly; the school contacted his mother. Afraid of returning to the school after the summer break, the boy eventually told his mother what had happened. She duly informed the school and the state police.

The case was given to Lauretano, who'd handled sexual abuse allegations at the nearby Indian Mountain School, where the victims won civil damages. Because of the delay in reporting, there was no physical evidence, but Lauretano conducted many interviews. The boy had been interviewed several times, but the police insisted on yet another interview. So Lauretano employed licensed clinical social worker and therapist Kym Crown to videotape an interview.

The *Hartford Courant* provided in-depth coverage. The social worker's report stated: "He appeared to state only what he was absolutely sure about. It is believed he is telling the truth about how much he knows and about what happened ... It is believed that [the boy] was severely traumatized by this ordeal."

And a medical report noted: "his severe ... anxiety, his new onset of sleep disturbances and other symptoms support the diagnosis of sexual abuse as well as suggest that [the] victim is manifesting symptoms of post-traumatic stress disorder."

Lauretano obtained a search warrant. The office of State's Attorney Frank Maco told the boy's mom that arrest warrants would be issued. But Lauretano's arrest warrants were returned unsigned, citing spelling and grammatical mistakes. In January 1998 Lauretano was removed from the case, which was transferred to the Major Crime Squad.

From then on, the case turned *not* on a coerced confession—as in the Reilly and Solberg cases—but on a claim of coerced *recantation*. The police asked the mother and son to come to the Bridgeport barracks on February 28—one year after the alleged attack. When they arrived, the police offered to give the boy a tour of the buildings while the mother waited. Instead, without his mom's knowledge, the boy was interrogated alone for close to four hours by three detectives who claimed to have no knowledge of the therapist's videotaped interview. No recording was made, but at the end of the interrogation the boy changed his statement in writing. It was now phrased *hypothetically*, as a *possible scenario* put forward by the police.

"If it is proven that a crime was not committed on the night of Feb. 28 (1997), I will recant the statements that I have made ... the stress of the harassment ... could have made me think the incident occurred or it would have been a very vivid dream."

He was returned to his mom in tears and begged to leave. A detective insisted that she, too, sign the statement. Shortly before arriving home she parked to talk to the boy, but he fled. He came home later, ran off again crying, finally returning later that evening. Psychologically traumatized, he began suffering seizures and was hospitalized for several weeks. His mother complained, to no avail.

"My son said he wanted to speak to me. They wouldn't let him see me ... If my little black son had raped and sodomized two white boys, he would have been locked up a long time ago," reported the *Republican American* and *Litchfield County Times*.

The police conducted an internal affairs investigation and released their report the day before Thanksgiving 1998, claiming the boy's mother had "shown a tendency to slant issues so that they are postured in the best possible manner for her complaint or possible lawsuit."

Police Commissioner John Connelly and State's Attorney Maco stated the boy's rights had not been violated.

The case was closed.

The Hotchkiss School allowed the alleged perpetrators to remain but told the boy "regretfully" not to return. The school guarded its secrets well. Two decades after this episode, the *New York Times* would report that over the course of three decades seven staff members abused at least sixteen students. School administrators, although repeatedly informed of the allegations, failed to take action. One name popped out at me: Dr Peter Gott, the school's medical director from 1972 to 2005. Female students who consulted him claimed that he insisted they remove their clothes and then molested them. Well, Dr Gott indubitably demystified the God image of doctors.

The African-American student's plight faded from the public eye. The scholarship program wouldn't allow him to transfer his scholarship, so he returned to the public school system.

Ruminating about this case, I recalled a statement from Barthel's book on the Reilly affair. "I think that because of what happened to Peter, it won't happen to anyone again," a local woman had said. She was referring to the support committee for Reilly and the ensuing publicity, which allowed justice to prevail after a long battle. But she was wrong. Reilly's mom may have been an outsider, but he was a local, raised in the area, and had local support. The African-American boy was an outsider, quickly forgotten.

Local newspapers replaced his story with that of the brave policeman confronting police malpractice. After a suspension and a transfer to another barracks, Lauretano was finally reinstated as resident trooper in 2002, retiring in early 2011, a local hero, before his tenure as selectman.

Since he was intimately acquainted with problems within the state police, surely he would want to help me, I hoped. I drove to the Salisbury Town Hall to speak to him. A small group of town employees clustered in the lobby. Detective Sorrento, who'd assisted on the initial investigation into Daddy's disappearance, was leaning against a wall, coffee cup in hand, laughing with some women. He recognized me. Smile in place, his eyes surveilled me as I crossed the small lobby. I went down the corridor, found the selectman in his office and, greeting him, sat down in front of his desk. He knew about Daddy's case; he had interviewed the Taconic Road witness.

"I always advise people to follow the money."

"What money? No money is missing. The only thing missing is my father!"

The discussion foundered. His eyes gazed behind me. I turned around towards the open door. There stood the detective, lounging against the door frame, still holding his coffee cup. Lingering, he chatted with the selectman. They batted words back and forth, making small talk, seemingly oblivious of my presence. I waited silently, my heart sinking. Finally, I gave up and left, the two men still chatting. Later, I tried following up, leaving phone messages, sending emails, but never heard back.

• • •

That autumn I gave Daddy's file to a retired law enforcement agent who'd moved to Connecticut and was working as a private detective. Accompanied by a young man shadowing him as an intern, he visited me at the house.

He'd read the file carefully, he told me.

"I can't help you until the police get the phone and internet records," he said, confirming what I had presumed. He had no way to access them himself.

"The detectives who interviewed the last two known people to see your father would have failed Interview 101." He shook his head. "Believe me, I've seen many cases of police corruption."

"But this is as bad as it gets."

CHAPTER 18

Five years missing

Several newspaper articles marked the fifth anniversary of Daddy's disappearance. But their stereotypes about dementia were excruciating to read.

"There are so many variables it's impossible to say exactly when he wandered away," Detective Warren told a *Litchfield County Times* reporter in an article also carried in the *New Haven Register*. Although that first summer he had conceded Daddy could have been driven away, he now presented the "wandering" hypothesis as fact, buttressing Pamela's claim, even if tacitly questioning her time frame. "It's a disease that resonates with me on a personal level because several close relatives of mine have been afflicted with it," he added. "If he wandered into the swamp and succumbed there, it's possible we missed him." So evidence still didn't count for that detective who, in my opinion, was generalizing about a category of people based on his personal experience. To me, his swamp hypothesis was just another attempt to rationalize his initial failure to follow other lines of enquiry.

Pamela replied to the *Litchfield County Times*, and a month later she urged *New Haven Register* readers to think about "what could have prevented a man with dementia wandering from a home without a fence, a GPS type device and an extra layer of supervisory caregivers." She didn't mention that—if indeed he had left on foot—she could simply have gone with him.

Another *Litchfield County Times* article pushed *conservatorship*, calling Daddy "a confused old man who couldn't make it to the mailbox alone." It quoted State Senator Edith Prague, then chair of the State Senate Committee on Aging, who stressed the need "to alert the state when an elderly person appears unfit to live without professional supervision." By "professional" she seemingly meant someone state-licensed rather than a family member or private employee. "Somebody should have called the Department of Services for the Elderly. They would have sent in a social worker." Not only was she misinformed about Daddy, her statement was simply naïve; I've dealt with unimpressive state-licensed professionals and heard too many horror stories. I left phone messages for her but never heard back.

The reporters quoted a Fairfield County attorney—a purported eldercare specialist who'd never met Daddy, but who nonetheless claimed he "was the right candidate" for conservatorship. "If someone is incapable mentally, they should be conserved and protected ... I believe such a person should be conserved."

But Daddy was perfectly capable of expressing his own views up to the time of his disappearance—the notion that every person with dementia has to be placed under conservatorship is nothing but bigotry. I emailed the Fairfield County attorney: "Were you familiar with my father? Upon what evidence are you basing your claims about my father? The hearsay of journalists out to write a story?" No reply.

Responding to the *Litchfield County Times*, I stressed the need to collect evidence rather than rely on stereotypes and on the supposed accuracy of Daddy's employees. But I couldn't convey the anguish I felt that Daddy, so dignified in life, had been so publicly humiliated since his disappearance, denied a thorough investigation because of prejudice about dementia.

My student Eudora finished her Masters at York and returned to the United States, settling near New York City. On my visits, I would now look forward to meeting her in Manhattan at the Metropolitan, the Whitney and the Folk Art Museums. At her house, where I sometimes spent the night, I picked up Ralph Ellison's novel *Invisible Man*, which I had read as a thirteen-year-old. "I am invisible because people refuse to see me," writes the African-American narrator. "When they approach me they see only my surroundings, themselves or figments of their imagination, indeed, everything and anything except me." Daddy, too, had become invisible. People chose to see an old man with dementia, not a distinctive human being with a unique personality.

• • •

But at last good news. Several months later, as Obama campaigned for reelection, I learned that Daddy's case was being transferred from Troop B. On a sunny September morning the four-person Missing Persons Unit came to the house. A beaming smile on my face, I dashed out the kitchen door to greet them—Sergeant Todd Jamison, Detective Jim Buckley, Trooper Nina Carlotta and a fourth man whose name I never learned. Detective Buckley, tall, middle-aged with an attentive open face, trailed behind the others.

"I've been thinking about the phone records and credit card statements. We need hard evidence," he said.

"How long are the phone records available for?"

"Normally, about seven years."

"It's only been five. That must mean there's still time."

"As far as I'm concerned, we're all working as a team."

Once again, I had hope.

In the kitchen Bettina had prepared coffee and cake. We sat around the table, and Trooper Carlotta, a trim, thirtyish brunette, had a cup of coffee.

"What do *you* think happened?" Sergeant Jamison began.

Over the years people had volunteered their views that something unexpected had happened to Daddy that day—an accident, perhaps—and that he had been driven off the property and hidden, motivated by panic and fear of being blamed. The Hautboy Hill Farm search suggested that the police, too, were willing to consider that possibility.

I had drawn up a list of points.

"We still don't know for sure who was at the house that Friday night. Finding out who made that Bridgeport call and who they spoke to will help confirm who was here then." My words streamed out in a torrent. "We need to check the phone records of the two houses Pamela called on Saturday afternoon. Someone—maybe Pamela's daughter Dianna—might have called around asking for help. We need Jane's *landline* record for that Saturday to see if she received a call from one of Pamela's relatives, as she claimed."

Bettina's friend Eddie, a medical examiner in another state, had speculated that the absence of evidence above ground suggested Daddy's body might be hidden; they had discussed the possibility of submersion. Bettina mentioned Amelia's email claiming to have Nelly's payment for the hours Pamela worked the weekend of the disappearance. By Pamela's own account she had been too busy to work Sunday. Had she worked two jobs that Saturday, as Jane claimed? Did she return to Daddy's house, find him deceased and panic? Or, could Pamela have taken Daddy with her when she went to care for Nelly's mother? Did something happen to him there? Nelly's home was right near a lake and pond; Bettina urged the police to search them.

She wasn't the first to suggest submersion. The first year a retired trooper from Lakeville named Dean Hammond had contacted me about this possibility. He had been hoping to get a few divers to search some local lakes, but he's since passed away, and I never found out if he followed this up.

The missing persons team were silent, their expressions impassive, although I couldn't see Detective Buckley's face, obscured behind his nameless colleague.

I hid my fists beneath the table, my fingernails cutting into my flesh.

We were doing our best to cover the conceivable scenarios. This is what the families of missing people do. We go through all the possibilities to try to figure out what's happened to our missing relative. Not only is this practical, it's a coping mechanism. Discussing the emotional impact of living with a missing loved one, Pauline Boss argues that without closure, the grief process becomes frozen. Other specialists, though, suggest that imagining different scenarios and developing new investigative approaches over time enable families of missing persons to become active agents in dealing with the emotional trauma. In this sense, their emotions are not permanently frozen since their understanding of what happened to the missing person and how to investigate the disappearance changes over time. For me, thinking through the various scenarios and developing new search methods had become a crucial means of dealing with and surviving the trauma. However, while I coped with Daddy's disappearance on a day-to-day level, my persistent nausea and insomnia were testimony to my ongoing emotional distress.

Only if we could find and bury Daddy, would I truly recover.

Instead, I was forced to live with an enormous hole at the center of my life, like a crater left by a bomb. From inside that hole came Daddy's voice, crying out,

What has happened to me? Do you know what has happened to me?

I went about my daily activities, gingerly tip-toeing around the hole, always aware of it.

The discussion with the Missing Persons Unit was grueling. Our pain was palpable, in our cracking voices and grimaces. I still couldn't see Detective Buckley's face, but the other three wore masks of professional indifference that occasionally slipped. Were they sniggering? Had they no empathy with the families of missing persons? Were they so unmoved by the suffering of others?

One of my fingernails broke. Unfolding my hands, I saw the tiny curved indentations my nails had left in my palms.

• • •

The University of York had its own missing person case: Claudia Lawrence, an employee, vanished in March 2009. Back at work, physically, and emotionally drained, I spoke to an administrator about my case.

"I'm sorry for your loss. But, of course, it must get easier over time."

"Not at all," I said, unwilling to pretend. "It's not the same as a bereavement following a death. There's no closure."

Claudia Lawrence's mum told *York Press* reporters she would never give up trying to discover what happened to her daughter.

"Not knowing is incredibly hard and takes over my every waking thought."

Reading online about the Lawrence case, I stumbled across the story of Sean Toner, whose long-missing father Hugh Toner vanished in February 1994 from a County Armagh hospital in the north of Ireland. Sean Toner told a *Guardian* reporter that a missing relative was like "someone dying—you come to live with it but there is not a day that goes by that I don't think about the possibility that he may come back. The worst thing is not knowing." Sean Toner's hopes were raised with the discovery of a body on Saddleworth Moor near Manchester. Identified two years later, it wasn't his dad.

• • •

I returned to Connecticut during the spring break and arranged for the Missing Persons Unit to visit again. Three of them showed up, but not Detective Buckley, the one who'd stressed the need for documentary evidence—later I would hear that he had made headway on another missing persons case but then been transferred.

We sat around the kitchen table. Trooper Carlotta referred to a rectangular red rag that the state police had found a few years earlier in Massachusetts. It could have come from anywhere, and neither Bettina nor I had recognized it when Detective Riley showed it to us. Back then it had been tested for blood, with negative results, and sent to the DNA lab. Now the trooper claimed she had had it tested for DNA.

Had the lab never tested it? Were they still expecting to stumble across Daddy's remains in the woods instead of obtaining the documentary evidence and seeing where that led?

"What about the phone and internet records? Last year Detective Buckley said phone records were normally available for five years. Time is running out."

Trooper Carlotta replied that she found Pamela's account credible.

"But the four witness statements? Have you interviewed Dianna?"

"I haven't been able to locate her."

"I googled her. She's in New York City."

I was devastated. I had pinned all my hopes on a professional and committed team. The issue of trust in the police came up, and naively I mentioned my arrest. Their masks securely in place, they shook their heads, claiming to have heard nothing about it. They rose to leave. Here we were, at another dead end.

• • •

Six years missing

Months passed. No news.

The University of Basel awarded me a three-month visiting fellowship, which began in January 2014. I was glad to be distracted from my worries and to have the time to work on a comparative analysis of the Algerian and South African communist parties. Jack came out for a weekend, and we rode the colorful trams and old-fashioned ferry together. Later I flew to Algeria to give talks on my book on the Algerian communist party, published that year.

Then back to Connecticut to meet with the Missing Persons Unit at the Dunkin' Donuts in Thomaston. Driving there from Salisbury I got lost. Panicked, I arrived late, flustered, to find two members of the unit—Sergeant Jamison and the man whose name I didn't know—sitting in a booth, drinking coffee from Styrofoam cups. I slid into the seat facing them, ordered coffee and, trying to be polite, asked the man's name. He opened his mouth, hesitating. Jamison intervened, refusing to give his colleague's name.

"Any news about the phone and internet records?" I said, hopefully.

"They can only be applied for *immediately* after a disappearance when it's a question of finding the person or saving a life," said Sergeant Jamison, sitting opposite me.

"But Detective Warren got phone records in August 2008, a year after the disappearance. He filled out application forms stating reasonable and articulate ... arti ..." I sought the word, my Styrofoam cup in one hand.

"*Articulable* suspicion or exigent circumstances."

"Yes, that's it. Only he didn't get Jane's landline record or Matt's internet record for that day."

"The conditions are no longer *exigent*."

I pierced the lip of the cup with my thumb.

"But Detective Buckley stressed the need for hard evidence."

My voice faltered.

"The conditions are no longer *exigent*."

"What about the claim that Pamela was seen in Salisbury Pharmacy that Saturday?"

"That was followed up."

"What about Dianna, the first witness? As far as I know, she's still never been interviewed." I started tearing tiny pieces of Styrofoam off the cup's rim.

"We will do that."

"Pamela attended high school in the Bridgeport area."

"We know that." He sniggered; the other man nodded. I recalled I had already told them.

I tore more pieces off the cup.

"She might have been at the house Friday afternoon and received that call from Bridgeport. We would like to get the up-to-date case file. Bettina said you'd refused to release it."

Bettina was following this up with the Freedom of Information Commission in Hartford.

"I know exactly why you want the file," Sergeant Jamison snarled. "You want to get it, so you can criticize us. I can release it, but it will mean closing the case. If you want the case closed, I'll release the file."

"I don't want the case closed."

"We have to go. Are you leaving?" The sergeant rose, followed swiftly by his colleague.

"No." I stared at the table in front of me littered with tiny pieces of torn Styrofoam.

"I'm going to stay and get a donut."

Afraid they would close the case, I wrote to Dora B. Schriro, appointed in January 2014 with much fanfare as Connecticut's first woman police commissioner. I quoted the *Connecticut Police Officer Standards and Training Policy for handling Missing Persons Investigations*: "Inability to move forward in the investigation should not be a reason for closing a case." I expressed concern that the Missing Persons Unit had accepted the original flawed investigation uncritically and stated that I wanted an internal affairs investigation of Troop B's handling of the case.

I received a brief, cordial acknowledgement.

• • •

Seven years missing

I had been in touch with Jan and Bill Smolinski, and we made a date to meet at the Thomaston Dunkin' Donuts. I recognized them instantly from their photos in the press—Jan with a brown bob and soulful eyes and Bill, taller, his hair swept straight back from his broad forehead. Warm and friendly, they both stood up, and we hugged. It didn't take long to discover our shared observations and experiences concerning the police.

The Smolinski case was primarily under the jurisdiction of the Waterbury Police and had been stymied at the outset by the police failure to collect evidence and pursue multiple lines of enquiry. We had both been subjected to what I believed was police retaliation following our complaints about their incompetence. Jan had become a full-time missing persons advocate, but it was very hard to link up the dispersed families and friends of Connecticut's missing persons.

We promised to stay in touch.

I met with a reporter, keen to write a story about Daddy. Her article appeared in *Connecticut Magazine* that July with the headline, "Father's Disappearance in Salisbury Still Haunts Daughters Seven Years Later." I stressed that the Missing Persons Unit should follow up the still unexplored leads and put out a public appeal for information. I wanted the state's attorney to give complete confidentiality and immunity to anyone with information leading to Daddy's discovery.

"All we want is to find our father. I don't care about anything else."

The reporter hadn't reached Pamela, floating around the northwest corner, but staying mainly with a brother, and claiming to be a self-employed caregiver. But sometime later Pamela responded to her article:

"At the crux of the matter is the role Tom's mental condition factored into him going missing … I believe I am the one person who has felt the shock and disbelief the most since I was caring for him and after he left the home, with a small window of 10 minutes or so, could not find him."

Always the victim.

Demoralized by the lack of progress, I stayed up late one night, sitting at the kitchen table, the light a bright point for passing animals. Before going upstairs, I peered through the glass sliding doors, gazing across the dark lawn at the still darker Berkshires starkly silhouetted against the sky. Pressing myself against the glass doors, I felt trapped in a glass box, beating soundlessly against its glass walls, unable to escape my prison of loneliness.

I remembered the woman who asked, whenever she saw me at a seminar or conference,

"Any news of your dad, Allison?"

"No," I would reply, which she took as her cue to change the subject, never concerned to simply stop asking the pointless question or to ask how I was feeling.

"Isn't it time you moved on?" suggests a friend. She seemed to be under the illusion that since she had buried her parents and grieved, I should do the same.

How many times have people, convinced that they have my best interests at heart, tried to persuade me to stop searching for the truth about Daddy's vanishing? Those who don't know missing people and can't be bothered to imagine what it is like to know them. Their lack of imagination is all the more puzzling because everywhere I turn I find paperbacks, TV shows and films titillating us with tales of the missing. There is nothing more thrilling than a missing person case that gets solved—eloquent testimony to police perseverance.

All this time I had been making notes—my scratchings—and eventually I confided to a friend that I was writing a memoir.

"That must be cathartic."

"Hell, no! It's not cathartic, it's *excruciating*,"

"Doesn't writing about it make you sad?" asks someone else.

I'm already sad.

Many people mistakenly equate the missing and the dead. Most missing people may indeed be dead. But they are not *the dead*—those who lay where we have placed them, honored with accepted rituals. And there's no reason to pretend that they are.

Eudora understood, though.

One warm day we went to a Manhattan street fair. Browsing amongst the stalls, we paused and bought summer ponchos made of silk scarfs. Ambling on, she confided that her brother had vanished during the Biafran War. Settled in the United States with children, she couldn't go back to Nigeria to search for him. No matter that she rarely mentioned him; he still hovered, his fate a mystery, in the shadows of her mind.

CHAPTER 19

"How can you expect help from a corrupt police force?" asks an African friend.

I've told a few African friends I'm writing a memoir about the police investigation into Daddy's disappearance. Invariably, they reply:

"The American police kill blacks."

But mine isn't the tale of a police killing, nor of a coerced confession. It's the story of an old man's vanishing, police prejudice and abuse of power and the deafening silence of a community.

Eudora and I often discussed the American police, their propensity to shoot unarmed civilians and their disproportionate attacks on African-Americans. Her daughter had already cautioned her grandson, not yet a teenager, against wearing his sweatshirt hood up lest the police stereotype him, even though the local white boys wore their hoods without problems. The police are organized hierarchically into closed corporate bodies. All too often they operate without civilian oversight, and their thick conformist culture makes it extremely difficult for individual cops to rock the boat. She told me about a thirteen-year-old boy who'd enrolled in a police youth academy near her town. Tragically he had taken his own life; some people believed it was due to the pressure.

Would Connecticut's first woman police commissioner help me? In August 2012, when Dora Schriro was New York City's prison commissioner, the *New York Times* ran a feature on her Sunday routine. Like millions of Americans she loves gardening, cooking and police shows. While she was prison commissioner the teenage Kalief Browder was beaten by guards and inmates at Rikers Island prison complex and held for three years—two in solitary—without ever having been convicted of a crime. Two years after his release, he took his own life.

"Excessive bail shall not be required, nor excessive fines imposed, nor cruel and unusual punishments inflicted," states our Eighth Amendment.

Had Schriro been too busy cultivating her garden to notice that the boy's human rights had been grossly violated?

The Justice Department censured Schriro for ordering that an internal investigation report on violence at Rikers Island be sanitized by removing key details. A *New York Times* editorial claimed her actions gave "credence to the charge that the department historically protected and empowered people who were comfortable with misconduct and a deep-seated culture of violence."

What kind of message did her Connecticut appointment give to those state troopers who filled their reports with lies? How could I possibly expect her to ensure that Daddy's case was properly investigated?

• • •

After a research trip to South Africa, I spent the autumn in York, teaching, wandering in the countryside with Jack and preparing a lecture on Marxism and the Algerian anti-colonial struggle to be given at the Sorbonne in January 2015.

Back from Paris, I had a routine appointment before a cataract operation. I learned that I had bleeding in one eye, diagnosed six days later as wet macular degeneration. Shortly before my hospital appointment I had closed each eye in turn. Viewed from my left eye, a candle appeared to have had a bite taken out of it. I had assumed this was due to the cataracts, but, in fact, it was a symptom of wet macular degeneration.

After the first hospital visit, Jack raised his hand, jokingly asking how many fingers I saw.

"One," I said.

He lowered his hand.

"Was I right?"

"No. Two."

Speed is critical in treating wet macular degeneration, and the day I was diagnosed I received my first treatment—an injection with a long needle directly into the affected eye, which is numbed. Within days the large grey oval that had rapidly developed at the center of my field of vision metamorphosed. To my amazement, I now saw abstract images of faces and torsos—like Picasso's cubist paintings. This was Charles Bonnet Syndrome, the brain's way of filling in the empty space. But the cubist illusions soon vanished, and over the month my vision improved dramatically. I had three more treatments. The bleeding stopped. My sight was restored.

The very real and frightening possibility of losing my sight made my need to work on my memoir all the more urgent and was one factor in my decision to retire from my day job in July 2015. Anyone familiar with British higher education knows that the ever-mounting student numbers, never-ending administration and pervasive culture of bullying inhibit intellectual work.

• • •

Eight years missing

A short research trip to South Africa, then back to Salisbury. Bettina and I had agreed to sell Daddy's house.

In my heart, I didn't want to. The house had been my American home since I had begun my overseas wanderings. I had always been fond of nearby Canaan and had sometimes envisioned opening a café-bookstore on its main street. But the house was expensive to maintain. And I had never been able to shake off the fear of the police since my arrest. Having experienced their arbitrary abuse of power, I still suffered the physical and psychological consequences. Each time I crossed the New York State line into Litchfield County I felt a burning sensation in my stomach. I confided in Eudora.

"You've been *othered*," she said.

Friday evening, late September, I entered Daddy's house and saw immediately that something was wrong. Maufra's painting of the *Sacré-Coeur* was missing. In its place was one of Mommy's paintings, which had been moved from the hall where it usually hung. I contacted Bettina and John, our new realtor, to see if they knew where it was. They didn't.

A friend from Peace Corps days was with me; we had both taught high school in Ghana. She helped me scour the house, which had been vacant over the summer. There was no obvious sign of a break-in, but later I would discover that the garage doors were unlocked, and the spare key, missing. Who would know the house well enough to enter and take that particular painting? Who had such a grudge against us?

I knew I should call the police, but I was too scared. What if they sent Trooper Lowman, the man who'd arrested me? The idea repulsed me. I felt nauseous.

I had planned to visit Aunt Mildred in Georgia. She had left three phone messages. But when I called her, I learned she had died just days earlier. I was devastated. I had now lost my last aunt, my link with my childhood. Mildred, like two of her sisters, had died without knowing what had become of her brother. She had eventually come to believe that Pamela had been involved in Daddy's vanishing but couldn't imagine the police *not* investigating her brother's disappearance. There wasn't one conversation that didn't end with, "I sure wish they'd find your Daddy."

By Monday I knew I couldn't put off reporting the missing painting any longer. I called the police and made an appointment for a trooper to come to the house. In the meantime, I listed the missing painting with the Art Loss Register. To my relief I didn't know the trooper who eventually came to take my statement. He introduced himself as Trooper Winter.

"This is your painting?" he asked.

"Yes, my sister and I own it."

Bettina had moved back north and, since we had taken a chance on another tenant, had lived briefly in nearby Hillsdale, New York, before settling in New Haven.

Perhaps, the trooper suggested, Bettina had taken the painting when she moved to Hillsdale, which, as co-owner, she was legally entitled to do. Although she was back in Connecticut, once the painting is taken out of state, he explained, it's no longer Connecticut State Police jurisdiction.

"Do you think your sister might have taken it?"

"No."

That night Trooper Winter phoned Bettina, then called me and reported she had acknowledged taking the painting. I emailed her; she vehemently denied the trooper's claim and said they'd discussed *possible scenarios*.

• • •

Saturday, I sat down at my computer, and on a whim, googled the painting. There it was—on the web site of Fairfield Auction in Monroe, Connecticut! In 1983 a Paris art dealer had valued the painting at around $10,000 to $15,000, but it was now listed for sale with an estimated value of $3,000 to $5,000. I left frantic messages for the auctioneer, who later responded:

"Out of the office today. Maufra is still in the gallery. I'll call Monday."

Eventually we spoke.

The painting had just been sold for $1,700 to a French buyer and was due to be shipped to France that very week.

"But we have the provenance and ownership documents. I don't understood why you accepted the painting and sold it without those documents. Can't you contact the French buyer and explain the situation? Maybe he'll forego the sale on compassionate grounds."

"If this work was stolen, it will be returned to you. Otherwise, we can offer you no further assistance. If you have any further need to communicate with us, please do it through your attorney."

I told Trooper Winter I had located the painting.

"Monroe is close to where Bettina lives," he said. "This supports the idea that she took the painting, which is not a crime. Does she need money?"

"No. And the painting was auctioned off cheap."

Trooper Winter drove to Monroe and discovered that the consignor was, in fact, a Salisbury man named Zach who claimed to have found the painting at the town dump's swap shop. The trooper called Bettina with this news. Using the Freedom of Information Act, I obtained the recording of his call to her, made without her knowledge. In Connecticut, it is illegal for civilians to record phone conversations without the permission of all parties—but law enforcement personnel can do so.

Trooper Winter insists Bettina admitted taking the painting. Bettina is flummoxed by the painting's disappearance, especially since there was no sign of a break-in. But she doesn't recall moving it when she relocated to Hillsdale, over a year before.

"I just don't see how I could have told you that because I have no memory of it. And I have tried and tried to think of where I took it ... *if* I took it."

If. She stresses the word.

"But I can't think of where it was. I've tried visualizing it in that apartment in Hillsdale, but I cannot." She continues:

"All I can say is that the house did not appear to be burgled. They told me that the other painting was in its place ... so the most reasonable thing to me is that I took it. However, I just do not remember it. So for you to have completely extrapolated that I made a full confession is a little extreme."

Trooper Winter again insists she conceded taking the painting.

"I have no memory of taking it. That is the truth to the best of my ability."

"If you're telling me one thing last week and now you're lying, now you're messing up a police investigation, you're interfering with a police investigation, okay, and that's a big deal."

I gasped when I heard this: I had never heard a whisper that the police had raised the issue of obstruction of justice regarding Daddy's disappearance. But it seemed to me as if Trooper Winter was taking Bettina's refusal to concede as a personal affront. Was all this so that the police wouldn't have to investigate the theft?

"Don't accuse me of lying, okay," he adds.

She hadn't.

"Because in my position, I don't lie."

He then asks her whether she knew a certain Zach.

"No ... I've never heard the name before."

"Is it possible that you brought the painting down to the Salisbury transfer station, to this swap shop? That's where this man claims he got the painting."

"That's convenient," she replies dryly. "I would never have taken a painting to a dump ... I did not take the painting there."

The trooper called me.

"Do you know a man named Zach? He said he found the painting in the swap shop."

"Never heard of him."

"That's what your sister said. But once it's in the swap shop, it's abandoned property."

"Surely you don't believe his claim about the swap shop? It's preposterous!"

"He seemed truthful. He said he was more interested in the frame than the painting."

"That's ludicrous. The artist's name is on a brass plaque below the painting. Someone came to our house and took it. The garage doors were unlocked. Our spare key is missing."

The painting was due to be shipped to France as soon as the police gave the auctioneer the green light. I needed to buy time. Our lawyer asked the auctioneer to hold the painting. The Art Loss Register informed him it was stolen.

No, shot back the auctioneer—no arrest, therefore not a criminal matter.

But the owners hadn't authorized the painting's removal or sale, countered the Art Loss Register. The lack of an arrest is not proof of no crime: there are many cases of stolen items being returned to the owners without an arrest being made.

Connecticut, I discovered, has laws mandating the reporting of abandoned, lost or unclaimed property. The finder must report found property valued at more than $1 to the police within 48 hours.

At last, a way to get the painting back. The alleged finder hadn't reported his supposed find.

But Detective Sorrento, who was now assisting Trooper Winter, rejected this possibility:

"If he found it, it's his, and he has the right to sell it."

"What about the found property law?"

"For the swap shop?"

"But we didn't take our painting to the swap shop; we don't even have a permit for the dump. And there's no proof it was ever there."

What if one of Meryl Streep's paintings had been stolen and the thief, exposed, claimed he had found it at the dump? Would the police take his claim at face value? Would they apply the found property law then?

"Do the laws and statutes of Connecticut not apply to my family or does the Salisbury/Sharon Transfer Station Swap Shop have a special exemption?" I emailed the Office of the Treasurer.

"Without conducting an extensive review of all state law, we are not aware of any special exemption from state law for any entity," their attorney swiftly replied.

I forwarded this email to the head of Troop B and received an acknowledgement. They didn't close the case—or at least didn't publicly declare it closed.

So the auctioneer didn't ship the painting.

CHAPTER 20

The State Supreme Court finally overturned the Smolinski defamation judgment in October 2015, citing the First Amendment's protection of free speech. The court ordered a new trial, but the plaintiff withdrew her case. At least the court decision signaled some protection for families fighting for their right to speak out about their missing relatives.

That month I received the Missing Persons Unit report into Daddy's disappearance. How hopeful, how naïve I had been, three years earlier, when Daddy's case had been transferred from Troop B to the Missing Persons Unit. I had presumed that the investigation would be a joint effort. To my dismay, however, the case had been allocated to Trooper Carlotta, who struck me as the least experienced member. She'd signed the twenty-two page report the previous year, in October 2014.

The Missing Person Unit hadn't wanted us to see their records, and even going through the Freedom of Information Commission, it took Bettina close to a year to acquire the report. The electronic file that I received contained two copies of the report and various attachments, including a few early case documents, fifteen blacked out pages, thirty pages on sundown syndrome, which is associated with dementia, a two-page DNA report and three consent forms to search and examine evidence pertaining to the lake and pond Bettina had mentioned to the police. Two consent forms were signed, and one, unsigned. That suggested to me that the police had planned to search those bodies of water but hadn't followed through.

I spread the report on my bedroom floor in Daddy's house and began reading. The phone rang, and I leaned over and answered it. It was Detective Sorrento.

"Your sister has caused a lot of problems."

"I don't understand."

"She said she took the painting when she moved to Hillsdale." I sat up straight.

"Bettina said the trooper called her late at night and asked her to discuss *possible scenarios*. I'm sure they just misunderstood each other."

"It wasn't late. She said she took the painting."

"Well, he called me after 10 pm."

"She said she took the painting."

His words pelted me like stones. Somehow, I held my ground.

"People misunderstand each other all the time. They have different styles of speaking."

We talked in circles. He seemed bent on playing divide and rule and bullying me into agreeing with him. I stood up and began pacing, clutching the phone to my ear.

"Actually, I have a dated photograph of the painting hanging in our living room long after she moved out."

I sat down at my computer to find the photo, for once my brain working swiftly.

"You have a dated photograph?"

"Yes, last year I asked the realtor to photograph the paintings and email them to me. I'll forward it to you."

I sent him the photo and never heard back.

I contacted local papers about the missing painting. Surely, linked to a missing father, this was a human interest story. Most ignored me, but the *Lakeville Journal*'s editor flatly refused:

"We don't do criminal investigations, we trust the police, who are trained in this kind of thing, to do a better job than we might do."

"I never asked you to do a criminal investigation," I retorted, but was too demoralized to pursue the matter. Her stance seemed so different from that of the journal's publisher emeritus Robert Estabrook, who decades earlier had exposed the police mishandling of the Peter Reilly case. In my estimation, no one with first-hand knowledge of police practice could possibly maintain they were adequately trained in investigation.

Next I tried Salisbury's selectmen, who are responsible for the transfer station. I called First Selectman Curtis Rand, hoping for a little sympathy.

"I don't believe that our painting was ever at the swap shop," I told him. "It's not monitored; no records are kept. Can't you at least ensure that expensive items are registered with the transfer station manager so that there is a record that the owner willingly gave them away? What about putting a notice in the swap shop telling people about the found property law?"

"We are happy with the swap shop as it is," he replied.

I wrote to all three selectmen: "not only has our father vanished under unresolved circumstances, but now a cherished gift of his has also vanished." I explained that, by law, found property must be reported in Connecticut. No reply.

Bettina used the Yale Law Library to research art theft. She went to court, filed an application *pro se* to stop the painting's sale and obtained an injunction. I had just listed the painting with the Art Recovery Group. Its CEO, Christopher Marinello, was coincidentally in Connecticut and offered to help. He didn't waste time. Within days the contract with the French buyer was voided.

Zach relinquished his claim.

The Art Recovery Group emailed an agreement to all parties.

But who was Zach?

The answer was in our agreement. I was back in York when I received it. My head spun when I read it; I had to lie down. Sensing my distress, Margo grabbed me by the back of my neck as if I were her kitten.

The man who claimed to have found our painting at the town dump gave as his address a Falls Village house owned by one of Pamela's brothers—where Pamela herself had lived, and where a reporter had interviewed her about Daddy's case.

I just couldn't believe this was a coincidence. The police *knew* that house and others on that street belonging to Pamela's siblings. The day after Daddy's disappearance Detective Sorrento had interviewed Pamela at another brother's home on that same street. How could I possibly explain this latest development? Could the family have some hold on the police? Or was it something else?

What chain of events could have led to the painting winding up in Pamela's brother's house? Early that summer Bettina had stopped in Salisbury to check the house. She had made a quick trip to the local supermarket, turned a corner at the end of an aisle and come face-to-face with Pamela, talking to two hikers.

Perhaps mistaking Bettina for a local, Pamela tried to hug her. Bettina jerked away.

"Don't. You belong in jail," she expressed her opinion. Then she turned to the hikers. "Do you know what she did? She lost a human being. She lost my father."

Bettina finished her shopping and drove home.

Not long after, she recounted, a trooper arrived at the house and said that if a similar event ever occurred, Pamela would charge her with harassment.

Could Pamela have taken the painting in spite after her encounter with Bettina, I speculated? She was now moving between her brother's in Falls Village and her daughter's in New York City, styling herself as a caregiver and an end-of-life doula. Sitting at my computer, I googled the term. An end-of-life or death doula refers to a non-medical person who assists critically ill elderly people as they die. I sat there as this new information percolated through my brain. Is that then what had happened to Daddy, I wondered? I recalled her dream of finding Daddy's skeleton—was the truth slowly eking out of her?

Bettina recovered the painting. Success attracted publicity: unlike the *Lakeville Journal*'s silence, regional newspapers carried the bizarre story. "Mystery Surrounds Recovered Painting That Vanished in Salisbury" read a January 6, 2016 *Hartford Courant* headline. The reporter asked Selectman Rand about the transfer station's policy on missing property.

"When something is surrendered at the transfer station, it's surrendered," he replied, referring "other questions to the state police." Yet I had told him we hadn't taken our painting to the transfer station. Despite the Treasurer's Office statement, the Salisbury/Sharon municipality seemingly believed that it could ignore state law.

• • •

Recovering a missing painting is far easier than recovering a missing person. I finished reading the Missing Persons Unit report. A trooper seeking to advance in her career wouldn't find fault with work done by senior police officers, I reflected. And Trooper Carlotta was clearly ambitious. Checking the transparency.ct.gov web site, which lists all Connecticut state employee salaries, I learned that her earnings had risen from just over $51,000 in 2010 to—astoundingly—almost $139,000 in 2015—the 2015 median American household income was $56,500. Indeed, her bloated pay was standard across the state police force. Whether intentional or not, the inflated pay is a protection against whistle-blowing: very few people contemplating informing about malpractice would jeopardize such a salary.

The report rubber-stamped both the conclusions and what I perceived as the omissions of the original detective, by now a sergeant. And so many factual errors, starting with Matt's date of employment. It wrongly claimed that Matt's girlfriend Anna and Pamela's sister Amelia had been interviewed during the initial investigation and mischaracterized the depositions we had conducted at Detective Warren's suggestion as "a class action law suit."

There was no indication that the trooper had even tried to gather documentary evidence. This reduced the report to contesting claims—he said, she said. The trooper talked to Pamela—it wasn't clear whether in person or by phone nor why Pamela had agreed to be interviewed after so many refusals. She reported that Pamela stressed Daddy had "looked determine" [sic] that evening—the first time I'd heard this claim.

She spoke to Matt, but again, it wasn't clear whether in person or by phone. Matt said Daddy "didn't like Pamela and didn't enjoy being around her" and that when she arrived that morning, she seemed "distracted" and "visibly upset" about her husband. He blamed himself for leaving Daddy with Pamela that day. But, the trooper's report stated, he also maligned me and Bettina, claiming a neighbor had seen me chasing Daddy with a frying pan, for instance.

Really?

The neighbor's pine grove guaranteed total privacy for both families. The trooper had seen that grove, having visited the property. Why would she include such a claim?

Matt had "no explanation" about the Bridgeport phone call. However, for the first time ever, he "recalled running some errands before picking up his girlfriend at Wassaic but could not recall what time he left or exactly what he did." Yet another inconsistency about his movements during the critical twenty-six hours between Bettina's last call to Daddy and the call to the police. Evidently, the trooper didn't challenge it.

Pamela's ex-husband Steve was interviewed by phone. He couldn't recall exactly when his ex-wife called their daughter Dianna—"possibly early afternoon or possible late afternoon"—the crucial calls from Daddy's house were at 1:17 and 1:22.

The trooper tried unsuccessfully to get Dianna's contact details from both parents, claiming, wrongly, that Dianna "would have been a child at the time of the incident." But Dianna was almost nineteen at the time.

The trooper arranged to meet Pamela's sister, Amelia, who then canceled but agreed to speak by phone. Revealingly, Amelia recalled that she had been working for Nelly's mother that day and that *Nelly* had told her about Daddy's disappearance. If so, that would be well before Pamela's evening calls from Daddy's phone and her late night email to her family. So how did Nelly hear of the disappearance? Did Dianna tell her after speaking to her mother that afternoon? When Nelly told Amelia, did Amelia then phone Jane—as Jane had stated? The trooper apparently never thought to ask these questions. Yet this new claim about Nelly gave further support to Pete and Jane's statements about afternoon distress calls. Nonetheless, stressing that Jane's *cell* phone records showed no calls that day, like all the previous investigators the trooper overlooked Jane's afternoon *landline* calls to Pete.

The Salisbury Pharmacy manager was asked whether Pamela had been seen there on the day in question, but the employees who'd worked there in 2007 had left. Although at least one of them still worked locally, the trooper didn't follow up.

The report mentioned the witness who'd seen an elderly man walking on Route 22 near Wassaic. She checked the online databases for the remains of elderly men in Connecticut and New York. But no suggestion of searching that area with canines.

The report concluded Daddy "was having ... sundown syndrome" and therefore must have walked away from his home and presumably gotten lost. The records of Daddy's quarterly check-ups don't mention sundown syndrome. Nonetheless, Trooper Carlotta evidently felt qualified to make a medical diagnosis of a man she had never met, even though her diagnosis failed to address the key question of what had happened to his body.

It wasn't just the seemingly shoddy investigation that hurt. In marked contrast to all previous police reports into Daddy's disappearance, which, despite overlooking leads, were professional in tone and content, this report contained baseless and derogatory claims about the Drews that were traumatic to read. It felt so malicious. I sat on the floor rocking back and forth trying to soothe myself.

Bettina and I had opened our home and done everything we could to help the investigation. Yet, the trooper claimed, "throughout this investigation" we had not been "honest" or "forthcoming"—even though she had never contacted us for further information.

Moreover, she added, "despite this dishonesty or willingness [sic] to be completely forthcoming about information they seem to believe that there are conspiracies at work in the disappearance of their father." She expanded:

"I have found in my investigation that this 'conspiracy' theory has been belief [sic] of both [sisters] but neither have ever provided a motive behind this conspiracy."

And then:

"Allison did not inform me of the fact that she had been arrested for trespassing on her father's property by Troop B … I happened to come across the report in our database but otherwise would not have known. I have attached her arrest report to this report."

She quoted Trooper Lowman's claim that I had "felt" that my arrest was "part of a conspiracy" that had led to Daddy's disappearance.

Despite Trooper Carlotta's statement that I had never informed her of my arrest—why should I, after all?—I had nonetheless naively mentioned it to her and her two colleagues on their second visit to the house, adding that I'd been advised it was illegal.

By law, all records of my arrest were to have been erased. This is known as the *erasure statute*, and all the state clerks to whom I spoke knew about it. Indeed, when I checked for my own record I was told it didn't exist.

The erasure statute stipulates that when an arrested person is found not guilty or the charges are dismissed, all police, court and state's attorney records pertaining to the charges will be erased. The clerk of the court "shall forward a notice of such erasure to any law enforcement agency to which he knows information concerning the arrest has been disseminated" and "such disseminated information shall be erased from the records of such law enforcement agency."

Could it be that, inadvertently, some of my records hadn't been erased and that the trooper hadn't realized they should've been? Does ignorance of a statute and its implications absolve state troopers from responsibility for violating it? Civilians certainly can't use ignorance of the law as a defense. In fact, one Connecticut lawyer told me that looking for my arrest report in the police database, finding it and attaching it to the Missing Persons Unit report were all illegal acts.

Daddy had vanished more than four years before my arrest. What motivation did the trooper have for mentioning and including the arrest report, I reckoned, if not to discredit my appeals to the police to pursue the leads about his disappearance?

What about all the others who take accelerated rehabilitation? Was the illegal retention of my arrest report an isolated case? Or was it routine?

I understand that character assassination is a tried and tested police tactic to deflect attention from their own inadequacies. Quoted in the afterword to Connery's book on the Reilly case, Arthur Miller noted how swiftly "the question changed from who murdered Barbara Gibbons … to who was impugning the State Police." A Connecticut woman told me that after she criticized the police, they misused her family's DNA, hoping to prove that her husband wasn't her son's father. I knew of another Connecticut woman who couldn't bear asking the police for updates about her missing daughter, a sex worker, because of the taunts she would have to endure.

To discern this intellectually is one thing. But what is the emotional impact on the person when she or he becomes conscious of having been othered and when consciousness of pervasive moral corruption seeps into the heart?

Point by point, page by page, day after bleak day, I forced myself to go through the Missing Persons Unit report. It wasn't Daddy in the swamp. It was me, sucked in, and pulled under.

Was I going to drown in that swamp before I finished my scratchings?

Yet my scratchings kept mounting higher. I risked being buried by them. I needed respite.

I called Bettina's medical examiner friend Eddie.

"I've thought about this case a lot." His words gushed out. "It's very mysterious. Sometimes people go into caves and lie down. In that case the body would probably be desiccated, like a mummy, but it would still be intact and identifiable. I'd look for a place where he could lie down. You could also think about ravines. He could have fallen into a ravine. His body could be covered with leaves, dirt. It could be hidden for years. You don't know what his state of mind was that day. People often try to find shelter."

I scribbled frantically, trying to catch his words.

"Well, there are ravines, but I don't know of any caves … The area has been massively searched over the years. If he walked away, given his gait and breathlessness, he would have had to leave a long time before the employee said. She claimed he'd been missing for ten minutes." My mind returned to the canines' failure to pick up his scent aside from the back yard and conservation road. That's why I believe he was driven off—unless he's buried at Bartl's alert.

"Bettina's been very persistent," Eddie continued. "She's done everything rationally possible to find him. I'm sure the police are tired of it. They think, after all, it's just an old man, he probably died. How old was he? Ninety?"

"Ninety-one. Could he have been driven off and hidden?"

"It's very hard to hide bodies. They decay, they stink. If he'd been buried, unless it was deep, the body would very likely become unburied over time. It wouldn't be too expensive to hire a plane and map the area, looking for places where the vegetation is different from the surrounding area."

"Could you see that even after eight, ten years?"

"Absolutely."

"What about lakes or ponds? Bettina thinks he could be in either a lake or a pond near the house of one of the employee's friends."

"It's certainly conceivable he's in a lake or pond. But if he fell in, his body would have floated to the top. Then there would have been bird activity."

"Well, canines trained to smell bodies in water were flown over his stream and the surrounding area. They didn't pick up anything; there were no reports of turkey vultures. My father's friends and the people nearby kept checking for vultures. Do you think he could be submerged in water?"

"If he were weighted down he could remain submerged indefinitely."

"But would the woman have needed help?"

"How much did he weigh?"

"About 120 pounds, perhaps a bit less."

"Someone could easily drag a body of that weight and put a weight on him. I'd drain the water."

"Yeah, and there were wheelbarrows at the house. Bettina's been trying to get the police to search the lake and pond. She wants them to send divers."

"I'd drain the water or send divers. But after all this time the police become resistant to doing anything. You become the problem."

"Absolutely. I'm no lawyer, but I think we've been libeled. I'm not even sure how much the Missing Persons Unit investigated, aside from a few phone calls, an interview or two. The police finally released a summary report and a few attachments, with about fifteen blacked out pages. Most of the report seemed to be a summary of the original investigation."

"A lot of times these agencies are very resistant to releasing their documents. I've been trying, unsuccessfully, to get documents for a particular case, but may have to go to the Attorney General. That's the only way. You have to do what's rational, but avoid becoming obsessed."

"Well … the experience of people with missing relatives is very different from those who haven't experienced this type of loss. What's rational for people with missing relatives seems obsessive to others."

"The word that most closely approximates the situation is closure. You don't have closure."

"No, for sure we don't."

Obsession refers to a persistent disturbing preoccupation with an often unreasonable idea or an emotion that continually intrudes on a person's mind, displacing other aspects of life. Neither persistent searching nor considering the disappearance from different angles are necessarily signs of obsession. From the perspective of those close to missing persons, it's rational to search, no matter how long it takes, and as psychologists have found, it helps those left behind to survive emotionally. Of course, my need to move Daddy's case forward had blinded me to the risk that Sabrina posed. But was I ever truly obsessed? The Dutch-French film, *The Vanishing*, concerns a man who can't stop searching for his missing girlfriend, becoming so consumed that he risks and loses his own life to find out what has happened to her. His quest, initially rational, became an uncontrollable obsession.

• • •

I filed an internal affairs complaint about the Missing Persons Unit report. I maintained that the report did not distinguish claims from facts, but instead presented claims and opinions uncritically and without verification. I stressed that the factual errors, the reliance on stereotypes about dementia and the malice towards the Drews had distracted from the critical question of what had happened to Tom Drew. I also argued that the investigating trooper and the sergeant who co-signed the report had violated the erasure statute. Internal affairs gave the complaint to the very sergeant who'd co-signed the report—by then a lieutenant—who "found that there was no misconduct on the part of any of the investigators however the case remains under review."

A decade earlier Attorney General Richard Blumenthal and the New York State Police conducted a thirteen-month investigation into the

Connecticut State Police internal affairs division. Their report found "that many investigations of complaints against state troopers were incomplete and inadequate."

Had anything changed?

My complaint was passed to another sergeant who, as far as I know, didn't follow up. I wrote to Chief State's Attorney Kevin Kane asking for a copy of the internal affairs procedures and requesting that my complaint about the Missing Persons Unit report be addressed and that all leads into Daddy's disappearance be investigated. His office referred the matter to State's Attorney David Shepack, in post since 2003. Unlike other states, Connecticut's thirteen state's attorneys—dubbed the thirteen apostles by state employees—are not subject to public scrutiny. Appointed by the Criminal Justice Commission for eight-year terms, they are accountable to no one. No reply. And no copy of the internal affairs procedures.

Daddy, what do you think of this country, where the police choose whom to help and which laws to break?

Allison, you're mistaken. You've travelled too much. You're thinking of another country and confusing it with ours. That place you've described is not my country.

No, Daddy. This is our country now. It may have always been so for others. But now we, too, are the others.

Perhaps Commissioner Schriro had been so engrossed in her work that she had been unaware of her troopers' actions concerning the erasure statute. But just before Christmas she made time for a photo opportunity with the Troop B barracks personnel. That rusty neon State Police sign out front had been refurbished thanks to the lieutenant's initiative and local generosity.

"You have to respect history. To know history is to know where you're going," she expounded.

The *Lakeville Journal* ran that story.

CHAPTER 21

I no longer speak unless spoken to. How in awe I am of women who spontaneously, skillfully voice well-crafted arguments. I am at a loss with words. How can I possibly verbalize my feelings about what has happened? The words form in my head, swirling around so swiftly that they strike my skull, splitting into syllables and shattering into letters that slide down the slopes of my brain. My mouth is muzzled by an invisible bandage that I cannot budge. The *zwerver*'s life, the wanderer's journey that I began with my first voyage to South Africa, full of the zest to explore and learn, has long been a trap. Mute, mired on my own in a wanderer's track leading nowhere, I belong nowhere.

The community where Daddy spent his last twenty-five years guards its silence like precious treasure. It is a community of complicity, each generation forgetting past injustices, past police misconduct. They want to bury Daddy with silence. But I won't let them.

I want to bury him with soil.

So I continue searching, soundlessly, to assert Daddy's humanity, so cruelly trampled by the police and the town.

Jack, my beloved friend, inexplicably broke off contact. Thus ended the relationship that had been the center of my life for twenty-five years. No explanation, not even a good-bye. Had I known that the last time we walked on Spaunton Moor would be the last time, would I have wept then as I am weeping now?

A missing father. A missing best friend. It was as if a giant had grabbed me by my shoulders, lifted me up in the air and given me a good shaking, setting me down so forcefully, my head jarred, my vision blurred, that my body struggled to stand upright. That sensation hit me, shook me throughout the following days, weeks, months and more months. I had long lived with a submerged sense of nausea. But now waves of nausea arrived out of the blue, swelling and slowly dissipating, their unpredictable arrival all the more distressing.

A fog descended around me. I stumbled into a viscous substance, scarcely able to lift my legs to leave my bed. I was trapped in the glutinous material, like a fly tangled in a sticky spider's web. The giant would suddenly seize me again, shaking and dropping me, leaving my brain rocking back and forth in my head, my mind so crowded with these absent figures that it scarcely had space for those close by.

But Margo needed me. She was well past pensionable age. Her heart muscle had deteriorated; her heartbeat was irregular; she lay lethargically and toppled when she walked. The vet said she would be lucky to last a few months. I gave her pills in butter and, holding her in the crook of my arm like a baby, tempted her with pâté. Her eyes focused on me with that particular brightness of babies being fed. After she ate, I wiped her face and body with a damp cloth. But she continued losing weight, and one evening she wouldn't even chew. She eventually swallowed some chicken and lay resting in the garden. Then we watched TV together.

Later, I carried Margo upstairs, and she slept at the foot of the bed, as usual. I woke at 4 am. Margo had cried out. Carefully, I put my hand on her rib cage. It moved gently up and down; her breathing seemed stable. Later, another cry. I fetched her pills and poured a tiny vial of water slowly, gently down her throat as she carefully observed me, eyes wide open. Then I placed her on my chest. We lay like that for several hours, my arms embracing her, as the sky lightened. Suddenly she began jerking, convulsing for many seconds, then another cry, and arching her back, craning her neck up, gazing into my eyes, she gasped spasmodically, "huh, huh, huh," three breaths.

Resting her little head on my chest, she quieted down, and I stroked her softly. A while later I set her gently beside me on the bed. We lay facing each other, peacefully. I must have dozed. I opened my eyes at about eight am and reached out to check Margo. She was soft and warm. But my hand could no longer feel her chest moving up and down. She was no longer breathing. Her heart had stopped; mine was breaking.

Most cats hide when their end is near. But Margo had chosen to spend her final moments with me. That, her total trust, was her greatest gift to me. I lay with her for some time, cuddling her, murmuring "I love my little girl" into her ear.

Later, I cleaned her, fluffed up her long hair with the blow dryer and rubbed her with lavender oil. She loved lavender and often came inside in the evening smelling of the lavender plant. I was anointing her body, the custom across the world to show love and respect for our departed ones, knowing that this custom is denied to the missing.

I carried Margo around with me all day, holding her on my lap as I wrote. She lay peacefully, as if sleeping. That night I wrapped her in a small blanket, her little head exposed, and, as usual, we watched TV. From time to time I caressed her, comforted by her soft, silky fur.

In the morning, weeping, I took Margo to be cremated. My housemate, too, was grieving; her mum sent flowers and a note saying, "Thank you for sharing Margo with us." Several days later, I picked up her ashes and held a commemoration of her life with a small group of friends. My neighbor baked sweets and savories, and I served sparkling wine in my garden to honor Margo. I read poems, scattered her ashes around the garden and bid her goodbye.

I was only too aware of being able to dignify Margo's remains in a way I was unable to do with Daddy. I couldn't honor Daddy's wish to be buried with Mommy and to have her ashes and those of his Siamese cats scattered over his shoulders.

• • •

Bettina and I found a buyer for the house and had six weeks to clear it before the sale. Once more, full of sorrow, I returned to Salisbury, now draped in snow.

Obama's second term as president was drawing to a close, and the country was again readying itself for the presidential primaries.

I began packing and preparing my parents' possessions for storage, wrapping each item, each one a story about their past. Dusty, exhausted, I threw myself into bed at the end of each day. But I couldn't sleep. The field mice had returned for winter hibernation, nesting in the basement, the kitchen, the attic.

I heard them in the walls as I tossed about the bed.

How many mice were there?

It sounded like an army.

I recalled a summer day with Daddy when I saw his cat staring fixedly at a corner of the patio.

"What's Dandy looking at?" I asked.

"Come and see," replied Daddy.

I approached, and he lifted a flagstone to expose the cinderblock underneath. Nestled in fluffy pink insulation collected from our basement, a mother mouse surrounded by her nursing babies peered up worriedly.

"What should we do?"

"Leave them be," said Daddy, replacing the flagstone.

• • •

Despite the many years I had ferreted in the attic, I had never delved deep enough to find the boxes and bags squashed together in a far corner. Now, foraging, I discovered a large collection of Daddy's fashion sketches that I had never seen. Pen and ink sketches in black and white; watercolor sketches in a multitude of hues, little fabric swatches pinned at the side. Women's sportswear for all seasons, the styles changing over the decades. Some had been carefully placed in clear plastic sleeves and arranged in binders. Others had been stored in manila envelopes or crammed into brown paper bags.

More sketches squeezed in drawers, stuffed in plastic bags, secreted in envelopes, tiny sketches for garden designs in small notebooks, large sketches for needlepoints designs.

I uncovered a booklet of pen-and-ink cartoons of army barracks life titled *Tom the Soldier: An artist's diary in pictures*. Mr G.I. was credited for the men's costumes, furniture and interior decor. The last few pages contained sketches of Daddy's "exclusives" for his sister Martha Jo, complete with instructions on how to accessorize them. Alongside, was a newspaper clipping captioned "Baltimoreans on Bougainville" with a photo of three young army privates, including a slim, bare-chested Thomas Drew, kneeling before Japanese weapons captured at the Battle of Bougainville.

Sketches had flown from Daddy's fingers, just as words flew from mine. How does the human capacity for creativity begin? Sometimes it starts with a person's distinctive perspective, born of a unique set of experiences, flaring like a lightning bolt. Sometimes it is slower and begins with imitation and repetition. The process stalls. It stops. It starts again, proceeding in fits and spurts. Somehow, at some point in this process, the product of these efforts changes. It is no longer an imitation, but an interpretation. And in changing, it is transformed. Miraculously, something entirely new has been created, driven by the compulsion to express perceptions and emotions, and to interpret and reinterpret the world. Some creations are ignored, destroyed or lost. Their creators lose hope, their spirits crushed. "A striving, and a striving, and an ending in nothing." So wrote Olive Schreiner bleakly in *The Story of an African Farm*, a novel that I love and used to teach.

But others keep going. Their works survive and must be treasured and preserved.

Seeking a home for Daddy's work, I contacted the Fashion Institute of Technology and Parsons School of Design in New York City and Maryland Institute College of Art in Baltimore, where Daddy had studied before enrolling in the army. They all said yes.

In the end I decided on Baltimore, which linked the North and the South.

CHAPTER 22

Early February. The weather was icy, the ground covered with a thin layer of snow that thickened in the woods. I sat at the kitchen table watching large, feathery snowflakes caught by the wind, swirling, drifting gently to the ground. I recalled how Daddy had once braved an unexpected blizzard to stake a young tree badly bent by the wind and so saved it. How precious are our recollections of the disappeared, who, not honored by the ceremonies of death, hover as manifestations in our minds. No rest for the missing, who linger on the shadowy edges of our minds hoping and imploring us for those ceremonies of death. No snow falls faintly, softly on their graves, for they have no graves.

One afternoon I walked to the stream; I knew I wouldn't be able to see it much longer, nor drink its water. The snow's crust crackled under my boots. I heard the familiar gurgling and strode north along the bank. There, to my astonishment, half submerged in the ice-crusted water was an upside down cast iron bathtub. I pushed and pushed but couldn't budge it.

Could Daddy's body be underneath it?

I called a local man who, hearing the begging notes in my voice, came out with a friend and lifted the tub with a chain. Nothing, just dirt. I told Otto about the tub, and he mentioned that cow herds used to graze there. Perhaps the tub had been used for their grain. Maybe that buried stone wall had once enclosed those cows.

My mind ceaselessly whirring, I began panicking about selling the house without having had it tested for blood. I found a private investigator willing to do the job. He and his forensic specialist came to the house to test with Luminol, a chemical compound used to detect trace amounts of blood at crime scenes. For its effects to be seen, Luminol requires darkness, which meant that the technician couldn't test the rooms with the large windows. But, putting on her white protective garb and blue shoe covers, she tested the library, the hall bathroom and the garage.

They hadn't expected to find anything.

But the Luminol tested positive for human bodily fluid—blood—on the blade of a hedge lopper in the garage and on the library bookshelves and the under-the-sink cabinet in the bathroom next to the library—areas that had never been repainted and that Pamela had mentioned in her statements. I saw the shiny illumination on the blade and the intricate splatter pattern on the bookshelves and bathroom cabinet—hundreds of tiny shining dots, like a sky swarming with stars.

Frantically I called the police.

• • •

Moving day.

Three moving men arrived, jovial, hard-working. The realtor pitched in to help. Two plain-clothed policemen appeared to follow up on the Luminol. The moment the movers set eyes on the cops their bodies stiffened, their eyes hardened. The policemen explained to me that Luminol gives false positives.

"What was the window?" one of them asked.

"What do you mean?"

"How long between the last time a family member spoke to him and the report of the disappearance?" The question the original detective had never asked.

"Twenty-six hours."

"Mm hum," he said, glancing at his colleague.

I followed them around, observing, asking questions, sweating with concentration. Using Q-tips the technician tested spots where they might expect to find blood splatter. The results were negative. Two women arrived to clean the house. The movers glanced venomously at the policemen from the corners of their eyes. Someone called out to me with a question so I left the two policemen on their own.

The technician tested a few more spots before leaving.

Those results, too, were negative.

The movers left. Daddy's friend Julia dropped by with sandwiches and juice. We put the food on plates and sat in the library. I was starving and ate hurriedly, then told her about the Luminol and the follow-up test.

"Pamela's always presented herself as the victim," I blurted out. "But that first evening, before the police arrived, she told Matt and Anna they all had to 'get right on this.' Did they make a pact? Did Pamela ask Matt to say he left later than he really did? Is that why he keeps shifting his time frame?"

"I've never believed Tom left his home on foot, Allison. He was just too frail."

"The police usually ask people to discuss *possible scenarios*. They never asked her to do that. They just accepted what she said. The horror for me is that if the cops had just done what they're supposed to do—separated the three witnesses, had them each write statements, checked if any jackets were missing, searched the trash—the case might've been solved in the first few weeks."

"Have you been to the nature reserve, Allison?"

"No. Pamela used to live there."

"I've been there a few times since your father disappeared. I always sense his presence when I'm there. I feel he may be buried there." I considered this. The reserve had several thousand acres; visitors use the trails and keep their dogs leashed. That left a lot of land to hide a body for someone familiar with the terrain.

"They never searched the nature reserve with canines," I replied. "I asked them to search an area in Falls Village, but they didn't. And they never searched Route 22 near Wassaic or the lakes where he might have been dumped."

"I don't know if I sense Tom's presence at the nature reserve because he's there or because I know Pamela lived there. You should go there yourself and see how you feel."

• • •

Months later, I would follow up Bettina's appeal to the Freedom of Information Commission for the documents from the Missing Persons Unit investigation. The Commission had ordered the police to release those documents. But the material she eventually received dated from 2007 to 2011, not from the period of the Missing Persons Unit involvement. I drove to the Freedom of Information Commission in Hartford to pursue the matter. Those appealing for information were given folding chairs in a hot, windowless room. Eventually, the commissioners filed in and seated themselves behind a long table.

By the time my turn came, my throat was parched. I asked for water from the jugs on the table.

"No!" exploded a commissioner on my left. The others swiveled their heads towards him. The commissioner burst out laughing. The others followed suit. One of them poured me a glass of water.

I drank the water and stated that I was representing my sister.

A commissioner interrupted loudly: was I a lawyer?

No, I replied, but she had asked me to stand in for her because she was ill.

I had informed their office and was following their protocol.

I had two matters to discuss.

Firstly, I had brought my laptop with electronic copies of the latest batch of police documents and offered to show the commissioners that the dates of those documents didn't comply with the commission's own order. I can only wonder if the police used this seeming sleight of hand—substituting the wrong documents—to cover up what my analysis of the file indicated was the Missing Persons Unit's woefully inadequate investigation.

But the hearing officer—a lawyer—insisted that the documents complied with the commission's order. The commissioners ignored my repeated offer to show them the documents and rubber-stamped the hearing officer's claim without checking.

Secondly, I wanted to examine the full case file for overlooked leads. Donald Connery had won full access to the Peter Reilly case file when writing his book. I used the Reilly precedent.

"In the case of Tom Drew's 2007 disappearance, still an unsolved mystery … the State Police may similarly argue—to deny access to its file—that the case remains 'open.'

"For my sister and me—the only persons willing to inspect the file for ignored and overlooked information—such a use of the word "open" means an absence of true openness to useful knowledge."

The commissioners disregarded the Reilly precedent and denied my request.

Still hoping to hold the police accountable, I would file a complaint with the Department of Justice under the Americans with Disabilities Act, Title II, arguing that the Connecticut State Police had discriminated against Daddy on the grounds of mental disability.

But in law, discrimination requires the timely reporting of specific discriminatory acts, and the delay in obtaining police records prevents that.

Nor was I able to interest the FBI in the case.

I had spent a decade striving and striving to get the police to follow up the leads they'd sidelined.

And I had failed. An ending in nothing.

• • •

But on my last afternoon, my last night in Daddy's house, I wasn't worrying about the future. I was alone, for once wholly in the moment, my entire essence concentrated on being in the house. I went to each window and memorized its views until the light outside grew too dim to see. I needed to seize those images and clasp them to me, knowing I would never again see them. Those woods, boughs and branches softly swaying. Leafless now, yet I could almost hear their leaves rustling. Those fruit trees, branches trembling, so fragile. Those silver elms, limbs arching outwards, so proud. Those pines, reaching skywards, so majestic. I stared at the Berkshires, inky against the darkening sky until mountains and sky merged, the blackness softened only by the tenuous light of the stars.

I spent my last night in the house lying on the floor, wrapped in a sheet and blanket, a pillow for my head.

I wasn't cold, nor was I lonely. The field mice rustling in the empty attic, seemingly aware it was my final night, murmured gently, a soft susurrus, as if to lull me asleep.

I felt the house curling around me, enveloping me, embracing me, protecting me on that final night. My spirit expanded, flowing into every single corner of my house of creativity, and I knew it could feel my love.

EPILOGUE

I dreamed I was back at Daddy's house and decided to go for a run. Heading up the drive, I saw a turtle. It seemed to be turning in circles, its little paws moving rapidly, and at first glance I thought it was in distress. Then I realized it was scratching. I peered closer. It was scratching a message about Pamela.

"She can't let go of her last day with Daddy," the turtle opined. "It must be weighing her down. She needs to talk about it. And when she does," the little creature conjectured, "that weight will finally fall away."

The turtle ceased its scratchings, extended its neck and turned its head to look at me.

NOTES

Prologue

There are several West African fables about tortoises and leopards. The one mentioned here is in Chinua Achebe, *Anthills of the Savannah*, London: Pan, 1988, p. 128.

Chapter 1

On the psychological impact of a missing relative or close friend, see Pauline Boss, *Ambiguous Loss: Learning to live with unresolved grief*, Harvard, 1999; Hester Parr, Olivia Stevenson and Penny Woolnough, "Search/ing for missing people: Families living with ambiguous absence," *Emotion, Space and Society*, 19, May 2016, pp. 66–75; *An Uncertain Hope: Missing People's overview of the theory, research and learning about how it feels for families when a loved one goes missing*, Missing People, 2012; Lucy Holmes, *Living in Limbo: The experiences of, and impacts on, the families of missing people*, Missing People, 2008, at www.missingpeople.org.uk. Aside from titles, all italics in the text are the author's.

Chapter 3

On the history of Salisbury and nearby towns: *Report of a Committee respecting the Lands of the Sharon and Salisbury Indians*, October 23, 1742, Yale Indian Papers Project; Paul J. Grant-Costa, Yale Indian Papers Project, to author, December 15, 2016; Salisbury Association Exhibit, *The Weataug Indians of Salisbury* and *Indian Land Transactions*, 2016; Reverend Joseph W. Crossman, *A New-Year's Discourse*, delivered at Salisbury, January 2, 1803, Hartford: Hudson & Goodwin, 1803, p. 9; Malcolm Day Rudd, *An Historical Sketch of Salisbury, Connecticut*, New

York, 1899; Peter P. Hinks, "James Mars' Words Illuminate the Cruelty of Slavery in New England," www.connecticuthistory.org; Allison Guertin Marchese, "Cannons, Crosses and Ski Jumps," *Main Street Magazine*, April 2016, pp. 35-37; Estaban L. Hernandez, "Italian Culture, Though Changed, Still Strong in Torrington," *Register Citizen*, October 12, 2013; Carol Ascher, *A Chance for Land and Fresh Air: Russian Jewish immigrants in Sharon and Amenia, 1907-1940*, Sharon: Sharon Historical Society, 2017; Dooling, *Clueless*, pp. 109-10, cited in the preface.

Chapter 5

On wandering, Jan Dewing, "Assess Wander Walking and Apply Strategies," *Nursing and Residential Care*, 13, 10, October 2011, pp. 494-5; Jan Dewing, "Wandering into the Future: Reconceptualising wandering? 'a natural and good thing'," *International Journal of Older People Nursing*, 1, 4, December 2006, pp. 239-49; Donna L. Algase, "What's New about Wandering Behaviour? An assessment of recent studies," *International Journal of Older People Nursing*, 1, 4, December 2006, pp. 226-34; Gabriele Cipriani, Claudio Lucetti, Angelo Nuti and Sabrina Danti, "Wandering and Dementia," *Psychogeriatrics*, 14, 2, March 2014; Rebecca Solnit, *A Field Guide to Getting Lost*, Edinburgh and London: Canongate, 2006. On voting, Pam Belluck, "States Face Decisions on Who Is Mentally Fit to Vote," *New York Times*, June 19, 2007. On stigma, Nicole L. Batsch and Mary S. Mittelman, *World Alzheimer Report 2012: Overcoming the stigma of dementia*, London: Alzheimer's Disease International, 2012, at www.alz.co.uk/dementia-reports-policy-briefs. State police records on Thomas P. Drew missing person cited in this chapter and hereafter are in CSP case no. 0700292668.

Chapter 6

Statistics on missing persons vary. The National Missing and Unidentified Persons System, www.namus.gov/, estimates over 600,000 people go missing each year. Kevin Kepple, Marianne Epstein, Lori

Grisham, "By the Numbers: Missing persons in the USA," *USA Today*, September 23, 2014, estimate 750,000 on a ten-year average of the FBI's National Crime Information Center database; Nancy Ritter, "Missing Persons and Unidentified Remains: The nation's silent mass disaster," *National Institute of Justice Journal*, 256, January 2007. Quotes on the Reilly case are from Barthel, *Death*, ch. 8, and Connery, *Guilty*, p. 1, and quotes on the Solberg case, from Savage, *Great Fall*, pp 157–8, all cited in the preface.

Chapter 8

The depositions quoted in chapters 8–10 are from Docket no. LLI-CV-07-5003061-S, Superior Court, Litchfield Judicial District. The divorce records quoted are from Docket LLI FA07-4006567-S, Litchfield Judicial District Courthouse.

Chapter 12

On the Smolinski case, Alexander Nazaryan, "Billy Smolinski, Gone Since 2004, Is Part of a 'Silent Mass Disaster'," *Newsweek*, August 7, 2017; Hearing before the Subcommittee on Crime, Terrorism, and Homeland Security, Committee on the Judiciary, House of Representatives, Second Session on H. R. 3695, January 21, 2010.

Chapter 16

On the East Haven police scandal, Peter Applebome, "Police Gang Tyrannized Latinos, Indictment Says," *New York Times*, January 24, 2012 and "East Haven Police Chief Retiring after Charges for Offices," *New York Times*, January 30, 2012; Dave Altimari, "Ex-East Haven Officer Gets 30 Months in Civil Rights Case," *Hartford Courant*, January 21, 2014; "Former East Haven Police Officer Sentenced to Five Years in Prison for Criminal Civil Rights Violations," *FBI New York Field Office*, January 23, 2014; "Former East Haven Police Sergeant Sentenced to Four Months in Federal Prison," *FBI New York Field Office*, February 12, 2014. On dispositions of criminal trials, John Gramlich, "Only 2% of federal criminal defendants go to trial, and most who do are found guilty," *Fact Tank*, Pew Research Center, June 11, 2019. State police records on my arrest are in CSP case no. 1100667730.

Chapter 17

On US criminal justice, Shima Baradaran, "Restoring the Presumption of Innocence," *Ohio State Law Journal*, 72, 4, 2011, pp. 723–76; François Quintard-Morénas, "The Presumption of Innocence in the French and Anglo-American Legal Traditions," *American Journal of Comparative Law*, 58, 1, 2010, pp 107–49; Glenn C. Loury, with Pamela S. Karlan, Tommie Shelby and Loïc Wacquant, *Race, Incarceration, and American Values*, Cambridge, MA and London: MIT Press, 2008; *13th* directed by Ava DuVernay; "13th: A conversation with Oprah Winfrey and Ava DuVernay," www.netflix.com. On the Hotchkiss rape case, *Hartford Courant*, January 31, 1998, March 14, 2006, April 6, 2008; Gale Courey Toensing, "Mom: Son made to lie about rape," *Republican-American*, March 3, 1998; Donald Connery, "A Question of Coercion," *Litchfield County Times*, April 5, 1998; *Sunday Republican*, April 5, 1998; *Litchfield County Times*, December 4, 1998; Donald Connery, "Scapegoat: Trooper Mark Lauretano and the Hotchkiss rape case," *Lakeville Journal*, February 25, 1999; United States District Court District of Connecticut, Mark Lauretano, Plaintiff vs. Arthur Spada, John Bardelli, Edmund C. Brunt, Timothy F. Barry, Frank Maco and State of Connecticut, Defendants, No. 3: 99CV 1077 (DJS). On the Hotchkiss sex scandal, Elizabeth A. Harris, "At Hotchkiss School, Sexual Misconduct and 'Missed Opportunities' to Stop It," *New York Times*, August 17, 2018; Report to the Board of Trustees of The Hotchkiss School, prepared by Locke Lord, LLP, August 2018, www.hotchkiss.org/uploaded/documents/Hotchkiss_FINAL.pdf?1534530340087.

Chapter 18

On stigma, Batsch and Mittelman, *World Alzheimer Report 2012*.

Chapter 19

State police records on the Maufra are in CSP case no. 1500-576405. On Schriro, Robin Finn, "Roses, Pasta and Police Shows," *New York Times*, August 10, 2012; Jon Lender, "NYC Prison Scandal Continues; Times Editorial Cites 'Outrageous Behavior' by Dora Schriro, Now CT Public Safety Commissioner," *Hartford Courant*, September 23, 2014; Michael Winerip, Michael Schwirtz and Benjamin Weiser, "Report Found Distorted Data on Jail Fights at Rikers Island," *New York Times*, September 21, 2014; Editorial Board, "The New York Jail Scandal Continues," *New York Times*, September 22, 2014. On Browder, Jennifer Gonnerman, "Before the Law," *New Yorker*, October 6, 2014, and "Kalief Browder, 1993–2015," *New Yorker*, June 7, 2015; *TIME: The Kalief Browder Story* (2017), directed by Jenner Furst. On macular degeneration see www.macularsociety.org/.

Chapter 20

On the erasure statute, Connecticut General Assembly, Chapter 961a, 54-142a and e (1), Erasure of Criminal Records, www.cga.ct.gov/current/pub/chap_961a.htm#sec_54-142a. On internal affairs, Connecticut Attorney General's Office Press Release, December 4, 2006; *Hartford Courant*, December 5, 2006; *Newtown Bee*, December 8, 2006.

NOTE FROM THE AUTHOR

Word-of-mouth is crucial for any author to succeed. If you enjoyed *Searching for my Missing Father*, please leave a review online—anywhere you are able. Even if it's just a sentence or two, it would make all the difference and would be very much appreciated.

Thanks!
Allison

ABOUT THE AUTHOR

Courtesy of Olivia Enstone

Born in New York City, Allison Drew divides her time between New York and York, England. She has a PhD from UCLA and is professor emerita at the University of York and honorary professor at the University of Cape Town. She has published five scholarly books on anti-apartheid and anti-colonial movements in South Africa and Algeria. She loves animals, rambling in the countryside and singing. Find out more at https://allisondrew.org/.

Thank you so much for reading one of our **True Crime** novels.

If you enjoyed the experience, please check out our recommendation for your next great read!

The Poisoned Glass by Kimberly Tilley

"A great read and a fascinating retelling of a long-forgotten murder,

that still resonates to this very day...

for anybody interested in the history of the Silk City!"

–Mark S. Auerbach, City Historian, Passaic, New Jersey

View other Black Rose Writing titles at
www.blackrosewriting.com/books and use promo code
PRINT to receive a **20% discount** when purchasing.

www.ingramcontent.com/pod-product-compliance
Lightning Source LLC
Chambersburg PA
CBHW071435080526
44587CB00014B/1855